ORGANIZE
YOUR LIFE

5 Minutes a Day Can
Radically Enhance Your Life

By Bestselling™ Author
S U S A N   S L Y

*"Not until we are lost do we begin
to understand ourselves."*

Henry David Thoreau

Dedication

This book is lovingly dedicated to YOU - a student
of life, a seeker of betterment and someone whom
I know, beyond a shadow of a doubt, is Divinely
created and has infinite potential.

Susan

Table of Contents

Introduction

Introduction

Let me ask you a question – what have you done in the last five minutes? Has it been productive or does it feel like another insignificant amount of time spent on doing something that also feels insignificant? Five minutes may not seem like a massive amount of time to achieve anything of substance; however, the most successful people in the world maximize those seemingly meager 300 seconds, whereas those who struggle simply let time slip by. For example, in five minutes you can burn an extra 50-70 calories doing a quick workout like those suggested in the OYL Life Hack section of this book. You can return 5-10 emails by using the techniques outlined in the streamlining communication section. You can even take your romance to the next level using the relationship hack tips. Yes, five minutes, when used to their maximum potential, can radically transform the key areas of your life.

If you are like most people, you probably feel as though you do not have enough time to get everything done that you want to, and need to, in a day. This type of thinking is what causes the average person to struggle. Successful people, conversely, understand that time is the most valuable commodity they have. As a result, they choose to master themselves by becoming more and more efficient, getting highly organized and utilizing straight-forward techniques, like those you are about to learn in this book, to get more done with less effort and in less time.

For years I have been teaching my students how to do more in five minutes, or with five simple actions, than they would have previously accomplished in an hour. Five is a powerful number, and in fact, it is mentioned in the Bible 318 times. The number five literally means God's grace. In numerology it can symbolize movement and constant motion, which is powerful when it comes to getting organized. In Feng Shui, five symbolizes change and resourcefulness—again, all good things for progressing to a place of structure and function.

In this book you will learn how to leverage the 5 Principle and become highly effective. You will be taught powerful tools to streamline communication, how to productively clear clutter, schedule, and much more. In the last decade, I have had the privilege to meet, learn from and work with some of the most highly effective people in business, including *NY Times*™ best selling author, Harvey Mackay, the late business philosopher,

Jim Rohn, fashion designer, Donna Karan, and others. The organizational techniques that have been learned from these multi-millionaires are found within the pages of this book. By incorporating these *Organize Your Life* teachings into your own life, there is no doubt that you too can create better results.

As a balanced living strategist, here is my belief – balance happens in moments. My objective is for you to have more of those moments. When we become more organized, we inherently have the opportunity to create greater balance. I know you want more in your life, and I want that for you too. I encourage you to digest these pages, do the five exercises at the end of each chapter and incorporate the five minute life hacks, found in the last section of the book, right away.

We are all capable of achieving greater results in our lives. It is my objective that this book will help you get to that next level, become more organized, efficient and live into the life of your dreams. Let's get started!

Susan

Chapter One
Why We Do What We Do

"Knowledge will give you power, but character respect."

-Bruce Lee

Your Personal Groundhog Day

Let's walk thru the day of the average person. Joe (or Jane) Average wakes up feeling exhausted, has hit the snooze button on their phone at least once, and groggily faces the world. The initial thought Joe or Jane has is, 'check my phone.' An important text or email may have come in overnight and it is critical. After this, a quick scour of social media is essential and then perhaps a check of the news. Now, feeling even worse than they did moments ago, they plod into another day.

If you are like Jane, you fret over your mile-long 'to-do' list. One of the largest studies to examining connectivity in the brain was performed by Dr. Ragini Verma and colleagues at the Perelman School of Medicine at the University of Pennsylvania. The brains of over 900 subjects, both men and women, were imaged, and among the interesting findings, the study illustrated that women possess more neural pathways between the right and left hemispheres of their brains. What this means, as my friend Dr. John Gray, author of *Men Are from Mars, Women Are from Venus,* suggests, is that women think in cause and effect much more than men do.

Jane is already thinking things like, 'What should I make for dinner?' She thinks, 'lasagna,' and then thinks, 'no – we had that last week.' Then her mind rushes through options, and she also thinks about what to wear today while also contemplating that it has been a long time since she worked out and wonders when the last time she and Joe had sex was.

I was once interviewed on a popular morning television show in Australia to promote my book – *The Have It All Woman*. The interviewer asked me about how women think, and I responded that most women are running through the grocery list while making love to their partner. He said that he didn't believe me. I suggested he call his wife. During the break, he did, and she verified that this is true. The reality is, and I am sorry men, that women are wired differently.

Back to Joe and Jane. Joe is getting dressed and thinking about whether his shirt is clean or not. His mind may be focused on an upcoming task but not much else. Jane is feeling guilty about a host of things, and although she is going through the motions, she is likely not very present. Both Joe and Jane go through their day getting quick brain 'fixes' like sugar and caffeine. By the end of the day, Jane's 'to-do' list is longer than it was when she started her day, and she feels overwhelmed and disappointed that she hasn't accomplished as much as she had hoped.

To subdue their over-taxed brains, they drink some wine and check their social media, bringing laptops to bed, returning emails and tucking in for a restless night of sleep. Both Joe and Jane feel unfulfilled - like they are missing out. No matter what they try, nothing seems to completely satisfy them. They both wonder if this is all there is. In Bill Murray's 1993 movie, *Groundhog Day*, the main character lived the same day over and over, becoming more and more frustrated until he finally got 'it' – the only way anything would change was if HE began changing. If your life feels like your own personal Groundhog Day, then the same holds true for you – nothing in your life, not how you feel, how you think, how you operate and the results you achieve, is going to change unless YOU make a change.

You Are In One of a Few Places Right Now

You are likely in one of three categories – the first being that you can completely relate to Joe or Jane. You are thinking, 'Susan – how did you know about MY life?' Numerous studies support the notion that we are not coping well. According to the American Psychological Association, 51% of women and 32% of men report regularly lying awake at night due to stress. Furthermore, as of 2014, both genders report that their stress has increased over the past year.

The second category you might fall into is that Joe and Jane are somewhat relevant to you. There are days when you feel overwhelmed, stressed out and unfulfilled and other days which seem to offer a greater sense of flow. According to a 2013 Harris Interactive Poll of 2345 Americans, only one out of three considered themselves happy. The poll also illustrated that as we get older, we tend to feel happier. Those who were newly out of college or in their prime spending years while raising a family tended toward lower happiness. If this is you, then my goal with this material is to help you have more days when you feel productive, accomplishing more with greater ease.

Lastly, you might resonate with Joe and Jane only some of the time, or perhaps this was you in the past. If you are in this category, then it is essential for you to read this work and absorb it. You are rare, and the world needs more ambassadors of possibility like you. Engage in this work as though you are going to teach this material.

The truth is that many people out there are stressed out about a variety of issues from health to finances. To compensate, they turn to things such as television, social media and other outlets to numb their day-to-day life. This only serves to fuel the feelings of lack of productivity, low self-worth, lack of fulfillment and low desire to contribute. If we know that our strategies don't serve us, then why do we do what we do?

What Are You Rooted In?

T. Harv Eker, author of the best-selling book, *Secrets of the Millionaire Mind*, wrote that our roots become our fruits; in other words – whatever we are rooted in will inherently produce some kind of result and these are either positive or negative in our lives. The question I have for you is this – what kind of fruits are you producing? Are they bountiful and delicious, or are they overripe and rotten? Chances are that if your results are not what you want them to be, then you are rooted in something that is causing you to produce consequences, many of which you are likely not even aware of.

Everything we do has a cause and effect. For example, the clothes you chose to wear today could have attracted or repelled a potential client, business or life partner, or employer. The food you ate today could have been a catalyst for feeling good or feeling like garbage, which in turn, affected your mood and your interactions with the people you came into contact with. Your decision to remember to tell your partner or your kids that you loved them today could have influenced how they felt about themselves as they went out into the world. The list is endless and so is the magnitude of how our choices affect how the world responds to us.

By making a conscious decision to change what we are rooted in, we automatically start to produce different outcomes. When we root ourselves in a foundation that includes conscientious organization, an environment that is free from clutter and chaos, and strong habits that maximize our time, we inherently yield more of what we desire in life. Changing our roots dramatically can be done in as little as five minute blocks (or five actions) performed throughout the day. It doesn't have to be all or nothing, and in fact, that kind of attitude is often what causes people to either procrastinate or undertake something that they will never sustain. By choosing to embrace change five minutes (or five tasks) at a time, you will permanently change your roots.

The Top Five Regrets

So what causes us to make the choices we make? Behavioral psychologist, B.F. Skinner, was regarded as the father of operant conditioning. Skinner believed that the best way to understand human behavior was to look at both the cause of an action and the effect. To change the behavior, one must positively reinforce a desired action or negatively reinforce a non-desired action.

I studied Skinner in university while completing a science degree in psychology. What fascinated me was the study of human capacity, and why, although we are born of pure potential, very few people actually achieve a fulfilling life, fueled by accomplishment. In 2012, *The Guardian Newspaper* published an article featuring Bronnie Ware, an Australian palliative care nurse who worked with patients in the last twelve weeks of their life. Ms. Ware chronicled the top five regrets of the dying and they were as follows:

1. *I wish I had had the courage to live a life true to myself, not the life others had expected of me.*
2. *I wish I hadn't worked so hard.*
3. *I wish I had had the courage to express my feelings.*
4. *I wish I had stayed in touch with my friends.*
5. *I wish I had allowed myself to be happier.*

Bronnie Ware's observations struck a cord with me. How often are we wasting valuable days (the average human being spends approximately 28,000 days on the planet) doing things that will not help us feel more fulfilled? Are we going to look back and wish we had spent more time on Facebook or watching must-see TV? Likely not. The honest, hard truth is that most people are wasting time doing things that will likely never help them lead the life they desire. This book, *Organize Your Life*, is about helping you achieve the life of your dreams five minutes (and five actions) at a time.

I have taught my students over the years that with clarity and certainty there is no overwhelm. When you can prioritize effectively, make better choices, say 'no' more often and live a life that is true to yourself, you will feel happier and much, much more productive. I do not want you to waste one more precious moment doing things that you will later regret. Starting right now, begin to ask yourself – 'Will I wish that I had done more of this or less of this when I am on my own deathbed?' It is a powerful question.

Looking at Skinner's work, it becomes clear that many people are choosing to live their lives in an appeal to please others. Whether it is someone 'liking' our post on Facebook™ or re-sharing our Instagram™ photo, we feel that this is a form of reward for being ever-connected on social media. In order to maintain a feeling of acceptance, we deem it necessary to watch the top television shows and know what is happening on the news every second, so we do not look like idiots. We are reinforcing our unsupportive behaviors due to our desire to fit in, while Ms. Ware's work only serves to support the notion that, at the end of our time, we will live to regret it with our last breaths.

Personality Plus

You may be thinking, 'Susan – I thought this was a book on organization, not on psychology or how my brain works.' You are absolutely right; however, my goal is to teach you real life strategies so you live a life not filled with overwhelm and regrets, but that you have more time to do the things that bring you joy and that your relationships, finances and health are at optimal levels. You will never maintain any degree of organization unless you understand why you do what you do. Psychology plays a major role in our behavior, and to create sustainable change, we must recognize and embrace the aspects of ourselves that are either sabotaging or supporting our goals.

In my early twenties, I worked in a psychological testing unit of a men's maximum security prison. It was my job to test inmates using several modalities to ascertain their fundamental personality traits. In that job, I observed a great many things, which only served to fuel my desire to comprehend why someone would make certain choices even though they were capable of appreciating an inevitable outcome, such as going to jail.

From working inside a prison, which allowed me to observe human behavior, I went into the world of fitness as a personal trainer, nutritional consultant and fitness instructor. Once again, human behavior was at the forefront as seemingly intelligent people would ceaselessly undermine themselves by working out and binge eating, or pushing their bodies so hard that they started gaining weight, or exercising and using recreational drugs, causing them to completely reverse the good they had done. Yes, sabotage was on full display as I worked with clients.

Having experience with personality tests like the DSM (Diagnostic and Statistical Manual), Rorschach tests, etc. in university, as well as my experience at the prison, it felt natural to apply what I had learned through my studies and observations to my passion of teaching people how to organize their lives. These tests offered people a glimpse into their personality which, in turn, offered them a form of guidance as to why they made certain choices which ultimately led to specific results.

With this in mind, I asked myself, 'If there were organizational personality types that were fun and easy-to-understand profiles, identifying various dispositions and their fundamental positive and negative traits—would this be beneficial in teaching people strategies to get organized?' The Greek physician, Hippocrates, identified four temperaments. Subsequently, others have expanded on these and related them to colors, animals, and so forth. In my observation, working with people over the years in relation to organization and productivity, two additional personas emerged.

Fundamentally, these personalities can be used as a catalyst for why we do what we do. They are born from our environment, our beliefs, and the reinforcement of those beliefs. If we can observe the best and worst of our personality when it comes to organization, we can not only catch and prevent self-sabotage but also make choices to reinforce ourselves when we are living into our best selves.

Having worked with tens of thousands of people in live events and also teaching my own classes, it has been through observation that these six personalities each have their own unique way of helping us, or hindering us, when it comes to navigating life. People have found these personalities incredibly useful, and it is my hope that you do too.

To exemplify these personalities, we have had an illustrator create cartoons that feature the individual operating at the extreme end of their spectrum; in other words – what it looks like when they are not functioning in their power. Audiences and students have found the illustrations helpful to pinpoint personalities and furthermore, create an avatar for the individual. You may resonate with more than one of these illustrations; however, I encourage you to identify which one is dominant.

Before we start, I want to emphasize that these are not gender specific. Although the characterizations have a gender assignment more for fun than anything else, each personality type can be of any gender or cultural background.

The Six Organizational Personality Types

Helen Helps-A-Lot

Helen has a tendency to say 'yes' to everyone and everything; in other words, she is a 'yes-a-holic.' At the extreme end of her personality, she will go help a friend move into their apartment while her own home if full of unpacked boxes. At work, she is everyone's 'go-to' gal. She does a myriad of tasks that are outside of her job description and is also the person who organizes the annual Christmas party. Helen is a people pleaser, and this costs her a great deal. One of her signature traits is that her health is poor. Outwardly, Helen is a big giver and someone who easily completes tasks for others even though her personal life is often in shambles.

At her extreme, Helen may be carrying extra weight, having difficulty sleeping, feeling slightly depressed or anxious. She starts projects but doesn't finish them. As long as she views something as sheer personal gain, she is not likely to complete the task. Helen is a great starter but a poor finisher in doing anything that she feels relates directly to her.

Helen may have experienced loss in her past and likely has abandonment issues. She feels that as long as she is doing things for others, people will not leave her. This often leads to feelings of anger and resentment when she doesn't receive the praise and recognition she secretly craves.

On the positive end of Helen's personality, she is very capable. If she decides to organize a room, she can start the project and not finish until it is completed. She is capable of creating a very loyal group of friends, and because she is willing to help and contribute, she is likely to attract people who will assist her when she requests it. Helen, in her power, is capable of great things and brings out the best in people, as her tendency is toward nurturing.

In business, Helen must be cautious of her desire to enable people by doing too much for them, as opposed to empowering them. Helen will also want to guard her schedule, making sure she takes time out every week to do something for herself. Although she might find that selfish, ultimately, she will see that everyone, especially those who give and give, needs time to recharge and regroup.

Helen can use the 5 Principle by examining all of the things she has committed to and uncomitting herself from five things at a time (more on how to do this gracefully in the coming chapters). Whether it is unsubscribing from five email lists or saying 'no' to five upcoming events, Helen can benefit greatly from learning how to use the 5 Principle to create less overwhelm in her life.

Harry Hoarder

Harry has a hard time letting go...of anything! At the extreme end of his personality, he may have amassed a significant amount of useless items which he, at some level, believes to have value. He tends to keep things that send mixed messages. For example, he used to be one hundred pounds over his healthy weight, and he has pairs of pants in every size just in case he gains the weight back. He keeps old magazines, newspapers, VHS cassettes (if you remember those!), unopened mail and a myriad of things just in case he needs them one day. At a deep level, being surrounded by so much 'stuff' creates perceived safety in the world.

To get his clutter under control, Harry can use the 5 Principle by choosing to deal with five items at a time. He can either donate, purge or recycle. Five is such a manageable number and easily sustainable. If he committed to doing this daily, by the end of the month he would have dealt with 150 items, which could be a significant dent in his prolific mound of 'stuff.'

On the positive end of Harry's spectrum, he can be a good archivist. If organized, he may amass a valuable collection or art or sports memorabilia, for example. When he gets hyper-organized, he can be helpful as an employee as he will surely be the one to know where things are kept. He might hold a higher level management position, or when he is truly in his power – run a business.

Harry would do well with a career that required any sort of collection. His desire to 'collect' could be channeled into many positive business ventures. For instance, if Harry worked in weight loss, he might become a collector of success stories. The desire to accumulate can be wrought with many pitfalls, but when channeled into a healthy outlet, it can provide great benefit.

Apathetic Annie

Unlike Helen or Harry, Annie has no drive to do anything in her life. She is often overwhelmed and exhausted and can't seem to get it together. If she has the energy, she makes 'to-do' lists; however, by the end of the day, the list is longer than it was at the start. She just can't seem to get anything done. Annie is a procrastinator and, unlike Helen, can't seem to get started let alone finish. If she is an employee, she runs the risk of getting fired. If she owns her own business, she is likely not making any money.

At her extreme, if Annie is in a relationship or has kids, her life is suffering. She likely has no sex drive, doesn't play with her kids and most of the time, isn't present at all. She may be mildly, or severely, depressed.

When Annie is in her power, she has the unique ability to say 'no.' Unlike Helen, who says 'yes' to everything, Annie, at the positive end of her spectrum, can simplify by delegating. Focusing only on the tasks that she knows are important, Annie can be very effective in management as well as ownership.

Annie's propensity to procrastinate means that her 'to-do' piles build up. To overcome this, Annie can use the 5 Principle – choosing to deal with things in small 'bite-sized' pieces. For example, if Annie's email inbox is 18,000, she can allow herself to deal with five emails at a time, as opposed to her tendency to deal with none. At home, she can give herself just five minutes to read a book to her kids as she likely doesn't do that to begin with. By working with the 5 Principle, Annie will become much more empowered, confident and feel more in control.

Chaotic Carlos

On the outside, Carlos may appear to have it all together – a great wardrobe, beautiful car, maybe even living in a luxury home. Unfortunately, at the extreme end of his personality, nothing could be farther from the truth. Carlos' primary life philosophy is avoidance. Like Harry, he collects things; however, the items Carlos accumulates tend toward designer labels and the material as he is extremely concerned about appearances, whereas Harry could care less. Carlos runs up multiple credit cards. He is first to pick up the tab at dinner even though he can't afford it. Underneath all of this is an extreme desire to fit in and be liked.

Carlos expresses his disorganization in several ways, from stuffing bills into a drawer so he won't have to look at them to retaining the sales bags from luxury stores as a reminder of his perceived self-worth. Carlos' many watches, belts, sunglasses and designer suits are likely well laid out like the many stores he patronizes; however, he is extremely disorganized in any aspect of his finances and may well have not filed taxes for years.

At the opposite end of the spectrum, when Carlos is in his power, he can be very charismatic, a great presenter and natural leader. When he keeps his spending in check and has the transparency to openly share his many mistakes, he can be very inspiring. When Carlos is organized, he is one of the most likely personalities to run a very fastidious office (it will always be decorated beautifully), and his clients will often have the wow-factor.

Carlos can use the 5 Principle in several ways. He should always give himself five days before making any large purchase, allowing himself to decipher whether or not he really wants it. He should also take five actions every day toward cleaning up his lack of organization. It could be calling out to creditors to arrange a payment plan, booking an appointment for debt consolidation, canceling some of his credit cards, and ultimately, finding other ways to create self-worth other than the material.

Obsessive Ollie

Like Carlos, Ollie is all about appearances; however, her tendency is not toward spending to achieve it. Unlike my book, *The Have It All Woman*, Ollie is the do-it-all woman! Helen will go to extremes for other people, whereas Ollie's motivation is all about what people think.

At her extreme, Ollie is obsessed. If company, or even the UPS™ delivery person, is coming, she will make sure that there are fresh vacuum marks in her carpets. On her white picket fence, one scuff is one too many. After the child who ran their bike into the fence is reprimanded, she pulls out a fresh can of paint with the intention to fix one spot. She then decides that the rest of the fence is out of luster and will go ahead and paint the entire thing. After all – what would the neighbors think?

In work mode, Ollie's desk is always immaculate. She runs a tight, organized ship. The challenge is that she really can't let go. Her life is about control. She is a perfectionist, and if life goes off script as it usually does, she does not handle it well. Ollie suppresses her creativity and may be prone to anxiety, lack of sleep and even eating disorders. Although to the outside world she may appear to be one of the most organized people anyone knows, the truth is that her extreme control creates chaos for her family, loved ones and co-workers.

At the other end of her spectrum, Ollie is likely one of the most effective people on the planet and can accomplish more in one hour than some people can in an entire week. She is deliberate, skilled and focused. She can unwind, relax and even put the cell phone away as long as she schedules it in. This personality type is very likely to have an extremely long list of accomplishments, and in her power, she is definitely someone you want to have on your team, work for, and get to know.

When Ollie is not in her power, letting what the world thinks can take over. She can benefit from letting go in five minute blocks. Whether it is running around and being silly with her kids, putting her feet on the (..gasp..) new coffee table and reading a magazine, or resisting the urge to cut the grass every day, Ollie will derive greater pleasure in her life from obsessing less and living more.

Militant Marty

Like Ollie, obsessed is an excellent adjective for Marty, but his world does not revolve around outward appearances. He is driven by numbers, data and other information to make sense of the world. Marty is very left-brained, spending the majority of his time thinking as opposed to doing. At the extreme end of his spectrum, he can be argumentative, dogmatic, skeptical and judgmental. Although his computer files are systemized and highly organized, Marty may have difficulty in relationships, health and other matters; you see, Marty is so in his head that he can justify almost anything.

In disorganization mode, Marty may have rooms full of 'stuff.' He would never declare that this is frivolous; on the contrary, this 'stuff' has particular uses which he is well-able to rationalize. Because of his modus operandi, Marty will generally gravitate towards positions that require his ability to generate data. He likes to be useful, solve problems and show off his intellect.

When Marty is in his power, he can transfer his left brain power to organizing other areas of his life. He has the ability to be very attentive in relationships and focused on health when he chooses because of his talent for concentrating on one task at a time for long periods. If Marty is to truly live a rich, fulfilling existence, he must see that there is more to life than spreadsheets.

Marty can benefit from the 5 Principle by making a concerted effort to do just five things every week that are experiential. Perhaps riding a bike, going for a walk with his love, laughing with his kids, going for a drink with a friend or going to a movie - all of these things can help Marty begin to organize other aspects of his life and find greater balance.

Five Steps to Course Correcting

Many people identify with one or more personalities and observe when they are operating at their best. It is also equally important to observe when they are sliding toward the non-power position of their spectrum. For example, with Helen, we know that if she starts saying 'yes' too much, she will begin to become exhausted, overwhelmed and may lean on non-supportive behaviors such as overeating, not taking care of herself and stop focusing on the things that will actually help her achieve her goals. Marty will begin to rationalize, find data and perhaps become argumentative instead of being open to new ideas.

We all have the ability to begin to slide. Once we recognize our primary personality, we can also identify the signs that we are moving away from our power. By being able to recognize when we are slipping, we can use the following five steps to course correct:

1. **Set an Intention.** Affirm, *'I am the CEO of my life,'* or, *'I choose to remain in my power.'*

2. **Be Willing to Resist Your Nature.** Whatever dominates our personality comes with its own tendencies that pull

us away from our goals. When this shows up, make a conscious effort to resist. For example, if you are like Carlos and you feel the pull of purchasing a new suit when you know you cannot afford it, resist the urge.

3. **Feel the Pain of Resisting.** Know that there will be pain. You will feel drawn to self-sabotage because, at some level, this is where you go. Allow yourself to feel it, knowing that, ultimately, this is the right decision.

4. **Ask Yourself What You Can Gain.** By resisting something we know is unsupportive, we now can look at what we have to gain. For example, if you are like Harry, and having a hard time letting go of something, contemplate the feelings of knowing that someone else can benefit from your excess.

5. **Take Action.** Move in a healthy direction away from the behavior you know is pulling you farther from what you want.

The next time you find yourself sliding into old patterns, use your personality type as an anchor. For instance, if you are feeling apathetic, say, "Don't be an Annie." If you want to spend money you do not have, say, "Stop it Carlos." If you have a strong urge to create a spreadsheet as opposed to making a sales call, declare, "Enough Marty. Let's get going!"

At first, resisting the urge to buy an additional item of clothing or hold onto that National Geographic Magazine from 1982 that you might use 'someday' may feel dichotomous to your personality; any new way of being takes time to ingrain in our psyche. By truly Stepping Into Your Power™ and choosing to operate at the most productive aspect of ourselves, we begin to transform our lives, thus changing our outcomes for the better.

Yup – It is Going to Hurt

Let me ask you a question – now that you have identified your predominant organizational personality type – what behaviors are you committed to letting go of right now? Where is your predominant personality sabotaging your life and your ability to get organized?

When I was eleven years old, I was obese. In those days, we had routine exams in the nurse's office. As part of this exam, all students were required to have a mandatory weigh-in. It was humiliating. With a snicker, the nurse declared that I was one hundred and forty pounds; I weighed more than she did. I was ashamed. I already hated my body, felt out of place as one of the few visible minority kids in my school, and now came the harsh reality – being fat further shamed me, creating greater separation between me and the other slimmer, healthier kids. During our P.E. classes, I was always chosen last for everything from softball to basketball. No one wanted 'Bubba Sue,' as they called me, on their team. On one particular occasion, we were running cross country, which at our school consisted of running up and down a dirt mound in the yard. There I was, fat rolls and all, huffing and puffing, finishing dead last. That was my tipping point. That is when I made a decision to change my life, a decision that required me to get organized and scheduled. This decision was a tipping point for me to begin to take massive responsibility for my life. No one was going to rescue me. People were great at pointing out the obvious problem, but it was up to me to create the solution.

The next day I woke up at five in the morning and decided to go out for a run. It wasn't pretty at first as I struggled down the empty street with the goal of running to our local Art's Centre and back, an approximate one mile round trip. I ran three hundred yards before my lungs started burning and my legs felt as though they would give out. The next morning I got up even more determined, knowing that it would hurt and yet willing to do it anyway. Eventually, I made it to the Art's Centre and back. I would go on to become an elite-level long course triathlete where the run was my specialty. I have been running ever since.

If you want to change anything in your life, you have to make a decision that you will not put up with it any longer, and that starts with listing out the behaviors that you are no longer willing to allow in your life from this day forward. Change is scary at times, and yes - it is going to hurt. You are going to want to revert back to your past behaviors, drawn by your fundamental personality type. You know that it isn't serving you; however, at some deep level, you have decided that it is comfortable. Guess what? It isn't really comfortable – it is easy on the outside, but it is costing you. It is costing you financially, physically, mentally and in all of your relationships. Yup – it is going to hurt at times, but the life you want is on the other side of that discomfort, so let's get started!

Organize Your Life Now

1. My dominant personality is:

2. When I am operating at my best this serves me because:

3. When I am not in my power, my personality shows up by:

4. Use the five steps to course correcting.

5. What behavior am I committed to stopping right now?

Chapter Two
Releasing Excess

*"Be Content with what you have; rejoice in the
way things are. When you realize there is nothing
lacking, the whole world belongs to you."*

-Lao Tzu

We Are Not Defined By Our Possessions

Years ago, just before I lost everything, a friend of mine asked me, "Susan – if you lost everything tomorrow, including your home, your business, and everything you owned – who would you be?" He went on to say that his observation of me was that I had chosen to define myself by my roles and possessions, quick to talk about the car I drove, the people I knew, and so forth. I was very much like Chaotic Carlos. He asserted that it was a false reality, and although it stung, I knew he was right.

My friend's question shook me to the core, his words vibrating through my psyche, 'Susan if you lost everything tomorrow – your business, your home, your possessions, your job – who would you be?' I went for a long bike ride to meditate on what he had asked. The answer that came to me was the word 'teacher.' Teaching was my passion. If I lost everything, it would be a great learning opportunity that I could use as a catalyst for teaching others. As if prophetic, about ten weeks later I lost my business, was locked out of all of my bank accounts, and wound up on my brother-in-law's sofa.

That experience taught me many lessons, the most important being that we are not defined by our possessions. It was heartbreaking, and through that process, I had to make some tough decisions. I had been burying my head in the sand. I wasn't organized, I hadn't learned the ability to get educated on the structure and function of running a business, I had not been responsible with money, and as a result, found myself in Toronto with three hundred dollars in cash, diagnosed with Multiple Sclerosis, no job, with only my faith to keep me going.

There was no question that refusing to listen to my gut had taken me to that place. Deep down was a realization that getting organized, taking responsibility and learning how to effectively make decisions in my life was the only answer. Looking back, I see so clearly how it all fell apart. The blessing is that it was necessary.

How can someone be a good teacher if they have not themselves had experiences that are relevant to the lesson? I had to learn that I was enough; I was not defined by my possessions, my job title, or anything else. At the core of my being, being me was enough, and that is my message to you – you are not what you own, where you live or what you drive. You are enough just as you are.

Are You Sending Confusing Messages?

For many, it is human nature to hold onto sentiment, even at the risk of sending confusing messages to the world. For example, let's say you have gone from a size eighteen to an eight – why would you keep clothes that are too big unless you had a conscious (or sub-conscious) fear that you would gain the weight back? Perhaps you are in a healthy relationship, and yet, you still have love letters from an old fling – what message does that send out? The answer, of course, being that you somehow are not fully able to give your heart to your new love.

Many people hold onto items that send mixed messages. What they may not fully realize is that all items in our home are a catalyst for some form of energy. If this sounds odd, consider a piece of music that brings back a memory for you. For me, if I hear Wham's *Careless Whisper*, I am immediately transported back to high school circa 1980's, slow dancing in our school gym. The B-52's song, *Love Shack*, reminds me of driving down Parkedale Avenue with a group of girls from high school, belting out the song at the top of our lungs. Other songs remind me of lost friendships, heartbreak and even the death of a dear friend. Music is a powerful inducer of both good and bad memories.

The same holds true of objects in our surroundings. If you have an old photo from a relationship gone wrong, every time you see that picture you will feel the emotions associated with that person. If you have an award from a job that you were subsequently let go from, you will look at that and feel both pride and anger at the same time. Any object that elicits a negative emotion creates confusion, and this confusion can ultimately create stress, anxiety and even chaos.

Here are several examples of sending confusing messages, garnered from my students:

- Keeping marketing materials from old businesses even though you are in a new business.
- Holding onto a vase, or some other decorative item, given as a gift by someone who subsequently hurt you.
- An email inbox with thousands of old emails that have gone unanswered.
- A wedding dress for a wedding that never happened.
- Jewelry from a partner that cheated and the relationship ended.
- A book about a subject that was never going to be read.
- Exercise equipment that no longer worked.

- Bins of children's clothing even though the person was finished having kids.
- Passwords that have an associated meaning that feels negative.

Items that create negative emotions stifle our ability to attract greater abundance into our lives; they also send extremely confusing messages about what we truly want. Having traveled to remote parts of Guatemala, Africa, and Cambodia, I have witnessed people who are happy with much less. I can tell you first hand that many people outside of the developing world are living with large amounts of excess, lives rife with massive amounts of surplus that would be graciously welcomed at the local shelter, single mom's group, or friends going through tough times.

One of my students, Nicole, a talented woman with a PhD, lived with extreme excess. Surrounded by clothes of varying sizes that she no longer wore, she knew that she needed to do something about it but couldn't muster the energy to get it done. Finally, at my urging, she took action and purged out bags and bins. Nicole had been out of work for a while and was having difficulty paying her bills. Within days of getting rid of her excess, she received a job offer, one that would allow her to work from home at a salary greater than she expected.

Nicole's story is not unique. This happens time and again with my students. As we go through this chapter, I would encourage you to release your own excess so that you, too, can have waves of good things chase you down.

Where Do I Start?

Getting excited about releasing clutter is an extremely positive move in the right direction; knowing where to start, on the other hand, is where many people struggle. The best thing to do is ask yourself what your top priority is right now. Has your doctor told you that you need to lose weight? Are you upside down in debt? Are you often fighting with your partner or another member of your household? Each of our top goals has one or more rooms of our house that is associated with that aspect of our lives.

For example:

Health- Kitchen/Exercise Room

Money – Home Office/Workspace

Relationship – Bedroom/Family Room

Once you identify your top priority, you will easily know where to start. You may be thinking that this sounds ridiculously simple and say something like, 'Susan, you have got to be kidding me. Are you saying that if I want to lose weight, I simply need to clean my kitchen? If I want to make money, I need to clean my office?' The answer is a resolute, 'yes'. Many of my students have found this to be the least overwhelming and most effective path.

I had a student who was on the brink of divorce. She and her husband had not made love in months. They were fighting all of the time. I asked her to describe what her bedroom looked like. Perplexed, she shared that her bedroom also served as a place for her to fold the deluge of laundry that she and her family produced on a weekly basis. There were piles of laundry, at least six overflowing laundry baskets, and a treadmill, which was used as a hanging rack. When asked how the room made her feel, her reply was that it was claustrophobic. I felt ill based solely on her description.

It was not surprising that her marriage was in trouble. When we walk into a room and feel a negative emotion that, in turn, is going to be a catalyst to suppress the hormones that cause us to feel happy, fulfilled and even amorous. Given the state of the bedroom, I am sure that my student's husband was feeling the exact same way.

I gave her one week to get the room cleaned up. She had to be accountable and post photos in a private forum. The results were nothing short of spectacular. Her 'after' photo displayed a room that felt open, liberating and much more soothing than the previous chaos. She happily reported that, miraculously, she and her husband had stopped fighting; even the children were calmer. She vowed to keep that room organized.

Like my student, you may have a challenge with your relationship, or lack thereof. In which case, start with your bedroom. If your health leaves something to be desired, clean out your kitchen pantry and cupboards. If your finances need some positive energy, organize your home office space. Over the years, many of my students have created instant results simply by releasing excess and clearing up the space that is associated with their biggest area of contention, thus freeing positive energy.

The Mirror

I teach my students that internal chaos is reflected back to us by external chaos. When we look outward at our space, we have mirrored back to us an amplification of something that is disharmonious within. Tradition teaches that when we work on ourselves, the world changes before our eyes. In creating this material, I asked myself if the reverse could be true – could something as simple as changing our environment stimulate internal change?

In 1971, Stanford University Professor Phillip Zimbardo asked a similar question. He hypothesized that taking on roles would indeed change our behavior, and that to reinforce the role, the individual would require the conducive environment. In a famous experiment, he created a mock prison in the basement of the university. Some students took on roles of prisoners and the others were guards. The study, originally intended to be two weeks, was abruptly halted after six days as it began to spiral out of control.

The students who took on the roles of prisoners became depressed, started revolting and acting completely out of character. The students who portrayed guards began to use force to control the mock prisoners, and within the first forty-eight hours, the experiment went much farther than Professor Zimbardo had expected. Although this work was intended to exemplify how roles could change us, I would further hypothesize that it illustrates how our *environment* can also change us.

To a much lesser extent, you can do your own experiment. Walk around your home slowly, and observe how you feel as you go into each room. Take as much time as possible—open drawers, look in your garage, car, closets, or anywhere you have storage. How do you feel? Do you feel your emotions shift from room to room? Ultimately, our environment influences our emotions, and if that influence is negative, how should we expect to feel motivated to accomplish anything?

Although you will start with the room that has the greatest association to your goal, I would encourage you to follow this with purging, clearing and organizing in any room that is a catalyst for negative emotion. As one of my mentors once told me, *"Your outer world is a reflection of your inner world."* One of the fastest ways to change yourself internally is to change your world externally.

The Monkey On Your Back

You may be a person who is somewhat organized, or conversely, you may be a person with a significant degree of chaos. Regardless of how adept we are at taming life's clutter, the reality is that, from time to time, there can be a monkey on our backs. Your monkey may be quite large – one of my students hadn't filed taxes in five years, or it may be comparatively small – your boss, or project manager, is screaming for a report. Either way, if there is something that is causing us a high degree of stress and demands that it get dealt with, then there is a monkey on our back; it will only get heavier as we procrastinate, so addressing it head on is the only course of action.

How does the monkey differ from the top goal? If there is a monkey, and there often is, it may align with the goal to a certain degree. In the case of my tax negligent student, she came to the course wanting to create more income. She hadn't filed taxes because she thought the bill would be too high. Interestingly enough, once she decided to dig in and address the taxes, she found that not only was she able to consolidate the debt, but money began to pour in.

Imagine that you have a monkey on your back, and it is causing you a great degree of stress. This monkey is blocking every good thing that could possibly come your way in many areas of your life. I had a friend who was in a job that she couldn't stand. She worked in a dark basement and had a boss who was unappreciative and demanding. Her co-workers talked about her behind her back; she was miserable.

In another area of her life, she really wanted to lose weight. She tried everything including acupuncture, detoxification, meditation and more. Nothing worked. In fact, she continued to gain weight. On the side, she had started a business which was bringing in enough money to cover her expenses. She also had contract work which was quite lucrative, and the contractor wanted her to do more. These two sources of revenue were enough to replace her employment income and would allow her to be at home with her children and have much less stress. Her monkey, the job, was something she just couldn't let go of. She thought it was her security blanket; however, it was more like a python strangling her slowly, suffocating her.

To many, the monkey in this story is obvious. However, depending on the size, it can take a significant degree of courage to deal with such a substantial foe. You may be like my friend, facing a monkey that seems like a five thousand pound gorilla, and for this, I wish you the strength to deal with it. The thing that I have observed time and again is that we make these monkeys out to be much larger than they actually are. When we procrastinate, we give these situations greater power, which like kryptonite to Superman, only serves to drain us of our energy.

In the Bible, David conquered Goliath with a slingshot. You may be surprised at how easily you can take your monkey down, using much less force than you had previously thought. The reality is that, much like Goliath, who was dangerous, your monkey needs to be dealt with because until it is – it will cost your health, perhaps your relationships and, in most cases, a significant amount of money. If you do indeed have a large monkey, start there first. The messy closet can wait – the back taxes can't.

Would You Pay $1 Per Pound?

Still having a challenge letting go of those old high-waisted Guess jeans from 1987 or the espresso maker with the burned out motor that you will eventually get around to fixing? Consider this - in America approximately 19 million households move every year. According to the Worldwide Relocation Association, the average household move cost $12,230 in 2010. When one looks at the cost to move a 3 bedroom home of 5500 pounds, it is approximately $5000, or about a dollar per pound. When you look at something and are making a decision to keep it or toss it, the question I have for you is this – would you pay a $1 per pound to move it?

3 Houses in Thirty Days

Ironically, in writing this book, I moved two times in thirty days and dealt with organizing three homes in a four week span. We sold our home in Canada and flew there to purge out anything we didn't want to bring to the U.S. Forget a $1 per pound – a move from country to country will cost a lot more than that. We then brought the things we truly desired to a storage unit while we waited to take possession of our new house. During this time, I purged out the rental we had been living in for one year. Although I am not one for clutter, my kids are a different story. Between gifts, school art, and clothes that they rapidly grow out of, as well as a continuous pursuit of recycling, donating and repurposing, we still had amassed enough 'stuff' to consider this a full move in and of itself.

My husband, my best friend and confidante, is not, how shall I say...as organized as I am. I make lists, I plan, I schedule, and these moves were conducted with military precision. Well in advance, I started donating and selling furniture from the Canada house. During our spring break trip, I continued to purge. My children were aware of their own duties for their first 24 hours back in the land of the North. My son would pack his Lego collection, which is quite substantial, and be responsible for all of the models which were already assembled. My girls would use tissue and newspaper to carefully wrap their American Girls and other delicate toys. Even though we had packers coming, this was no excuse for our children not to receive a first-hand lesson in releasing excess and taking responsibility.

For me, there was sleepless anticipation. I couldn't wait to get to Canada and start organizing, purging and letting go. As an aside, to give you an indication of my personality – my standard response to my husband's question of, "What do you want to do for Mother's Day?" was always, "Spend an hour re-organizing my closet," or "Purge my office." To have thirty days of purging, packing, and preparing was beyond exciting. Perhaps this is a little weird, but we all have the things that get us fired up. For me, a combination of organizing along with the absolute reluctance to spend a whopping $5 per pound for an international move was reminiscent of the excitement I used to feel on Christmas morning in expectancy of the delights left by Santa and my family.

Ultimately, when we are organized and focused, a task as daunting as moving is not a catalyst for overwhelm. In fact, any monkey, any room, any situation that requires de-cluttering and organizing can be adeptly handled using five simple steps. These are the same steps I used to deal with three homes in thirty days and the many monkeys I have had to wrangle during the course of my business career.

Let's Do It!
The 5 Steps to Creating Your Clearing

Step One - Identify

Whether you have a monkey on your back or an area of your life that is demanding your attention, it is imperative that you start with that room. The most common rooms tend to be the home office space, followed by the kitchen and then the bedroom. Take a moment and go within. Ask yourself, 'What is the room that I know requires transformation?'

Understand that, emotionally, it may feel extremely challenging to begin where you know you need to, as there is often one or more reasons why that room has gotten to that state in the first place. Avoidance and procrastination are common when we do not want to deal with memories that bring us pain. The faster you start to dig in, the better you are going to feel. My students often get organizationally obsessed, and once a room starts to look and feel better, they want to move onto the next one as they begin to see results right away.

Step Two - Prepare

As you purge any room, there will be three ways to release any excess:

1. **Toss It** – items that are broken, beyond repair, and that no one could physically use. I am a big believer in donating; however, sometimes when things are too far gone – there is generally only one option. Clothing with tears, deep stains or holes can be tossed also. Get cardboard boxes for your 'toss' items. Label the boxes meant for tossing with a marker.

2. **Recycle It** – old electronics, batteries, plastics, cardboard, paper (you will shred important documents), scrap metals, paint cans, etc. These are all recyclable. Boxes are ideal again. Label the boxes meant for recycling.

3. **Donate It** – the items that are considered excess for us are often very much needed by someone else. Over the years, I have worked with many women's drop-in centers

whose needs change seasonally. In my *Have It All Woman* work, our students worked with a shelter in Toronto. During the winter, women who used the shelter required coats and sleeping bags. They also required bras all year round. Contact your local shelters first and see if there are any immediate needs – you may be surprised.

I like to use clear lawn bags for donation, so I can see what is in them. I separate adult and children's clothing by gender. Additionally, I have family members and friends who are happy to receive the clothes that my children have grown out of. I write the name of the intended family on the bag which makes things much easier. For years, Chris and I have supported the Salvation Army and seen firsthand the struggles of people who are down on their luck. Children's and adult's clothing, gently used toys, and kitchen supplies are almost always welcome.

Step Three - Cordon Off The Area

I had a student who desperately wanted to make more money. I asked her text me photos of her home office. Trust me, not even Warren Buffet could produce in there. Boxes, papers, files, you name it – were scattered all over the place. It looked as though a hurricane had blown through. My student was obviously overwhelmed and didn't know where to start. After she took on step two - preparing, I suggested she divide the room into quadrants.

She used string to mark off four areas. I told her not to move onto another area of the room until everything in the first area was dealt with. In two days she had that office looking spectacular. It was much less daunting to focus on one quadrant at a time, and she was grateful for the suggestion.

In my class, I have seen photos of rooms that are so cluttered people cannot even walk in them. If you have a room like this, then you know that something has to be done; you just are avoiding it because the task seems so large that you are intimidated. Get prepared with your boxes and bags, and then cordon off the areas. Breathe – one step at a time!

Step Four - Use the 5 Principle

Let's consider that the average person is already overwhelmed to some degree. Carving out hours upon hours to clear clutter, although desirable, may ultimately feel like a delusion. Breaking things down into bite-sized pieces is essential, and thus, the 5 Principle was born. This principle is effective because it allows us to look at our possessions with objectivity, assisting us in making lightning-quick decisions on what to donate, recycle or simply toss. It also is the foundation for this book – could we deal with five things in five minutes? We absolutely could.

As you contemplate the items that are in the area of your home that you have chosen to focus on first, ask yourself the following questions:

1. Have I used this in the last five years?

2. Will I use this in the next five years?

3. Have I used this in the last five months?

4. Will I use this in the next five months?

5. Have I used this in the last five weeks?

6. Will I use this in the next five weeks?

7. Have I used this in the last five days?

8. Will I use this in the next five days?

FB content

9. Have I used this in the last five hours?

10. Will I use this in the next five hours?

If you have not used an item in the past five years and will not use it in the next five years, then you do not require it. I share with my students that there may be some exceptions, for example, a christening or wedding gown that will be gifted to a family member. Anything that you will be using within the next five years should go into storage, though it can remain at the back of the storage area. Other than that, creating a simpler, streamlined life means releasing those things that no longer serve us. Five years is a simple test.

If you have not used an item in the last five months and will not use it in the next five months, then ask yourself if you truly require it. This is also a great test as we often hold onto things and think, 'I might need this.' Anything that you haven't used in five months but may use in the next five months, like seasonal clothing, sporting goods, and other such items, should be stored away but easily accessible. Financial documents, which may not be required in the coming five months, should always be kept for a tax purposes for a minimal number of years which varies from country to country.

If you have not used something within the previous five weeks and will not use it in the next five weeks, then again, ask yourself – do I really need this? If you do intend to use something within five weeks, put it at the front of any storage area, so it is easily accessible. The same holds true of anything you may be using within the next five days. In other words, if you know you will be needing it, then put it where you can easily find it.

The only things you should leave out are those things that you need within the next five hours. How often have you been in a hurry and couldn't find your glasses or your car keys? Anything you might need today should be front and center. I like to pack my bag in the morning. My car keys, sunglasses, snacks, and wallet are tucked in, so I can grab and go.

I also teach my students to use the five-minute principle-tackling as much as they can in five minutes. Whether it is dealing with a pile of clothing to sort for donation or shredding old documents, it is incredible what we can accomplish in five minutes. Throughout this book, you will find ideas of how you can leverage five minutes to create greater ease and fulfillment in the primary areas of your life. Ultimately, when we realize our own power, and when we fully become aware of what we are capable of, there is such a high degree of accomplishment that, inherently, we truly step into our power.

Step Five – Deal With It!

Firstly – congratulations that you have made it this far. If you are reading right now and do NOT actually have piles of things to process, then STOP! You need to dig in and start this process. If you do have boxes, bags and piles, you are in the right place. It is definitely going to feel a bit chaotic right now, and that is completely understandable.

The easiest way to deal with everything is to move it to your garage or put it by the door. I suggest people write on bags and boxes to identify the destination, i.e., women's shelter, Goodwill, dump, etc. Take a moment and think about where you need to be in the coming days. Where are you travelling close to? Could you make a stop and unload some of these items? I like to pack my car with the donation goods so that as I go out to do errands or go to a meeting, I am forced to deal with them. I cannot stand a cluttered car, so there is a high degree of motivation to get things out.

There are services that will come and lovingly take your items. Many charities want your excess clothes and offer a pick-up service. There are shredding services. There are even people who will come and take your goods to the applicable places for absolutely free. Some of my students have goods that are damaged and beyond salvage, so they rent a dumpster. Yard sales can be a great way to make extra money and dispose of excess items if you have the time.

If you are overwhelmed, make a decision to deal with your items five at a time or in five-minute blocks. In the month where I sold my house in Canada, cleared out my rental in Arizona and moved into our new home, I used this principle. For example, in our home in Canada, we had a storage room where we had everything from holiday decorations to files and clothes that the kids would grow into.

I am not one to hoard clutter; however, as we had transitioned from a cooler climate to a warmer one, certain clothing didn't make sense. Admittedly, there was also a bin of sentimental baby clothes I had kept from the kids. The last thing I really wanted to do was tackle the storage room. It wasn't because of the number of bins; it was because I knew in my heart that going through the kids' clothing would be emotional. As a parent, letting go of certain items meant realizing that the kids were growing up, and although that is something to celebrate, it also creates a degree of melancholy.

I decided that I would handle the bins five at a time and then take a break in between to do other things. I enlisted the help of my mother-in-law and asked her to be ruthless. She is also a fan of the Salvation Army, so we both rationalized that these clothes, sitting in bins, could be very well-used by families in need. Together, she and I tackled the mountain, so to speak. The end result was several clear plastic bags of good-quality children's clothing donated with love.

Know that you can handle anything 'five' at a time. Whether it is sorting through boxes, going through photos, or whatever it is that you have to tackle – five is a manageable number.

Breathing Space

One of my students went through this process and had 28 bags to deal with. Although it was overwhelming, she felt so liberated at the end. Within days of releasing these bags, she attracted new clients into her business and felt great. Many of my students have, in fact, attracted money, opportunities and other great things into their lives when they released the excess.

We all require breathing space; it creates greater harmony in our lives. When we are in this place where we have released things that remind us of unpleasant memories, excess, or anything that disrupts our soul, we profoundly shift our reality.

You may think that clearing clutter is simply about tidying up a mess – trust me, it is about so much more than that.

Organize Your Life Now

1. Identify the 'monkey on your back.'

2. What is the room associated with this?

3. Where am I sending confusing messages?

4. Use the 5 Principle to Create a Clearing.

5. Commit to spending just five minutes at a time dealing with excess.

Chapter Three
Managing Ourselves in Time

*"Passion is energy. Feel the power that comes
from focusing on what excites you."*

-Oprah Winfrey

How Much Is Your Time Worth?

Time is the one thing we all have in common. From the moment we are born, the clock of our lives starts ticking. 86,400 seconds, or 288 X 5 minute blocks, or 1440 minutes, or 24 hours in a day; ultimately, the only thing that varies, from person to person, is how we use it. Consider that you have the same amount of time as Oprah Winfrey, Richard Branson or the late Nelson Mandela. What sets them apart from you? The answer is simply that people who are high achievers set a different value on their time than those who struggle to obtain an objective.

I had a student, let's call her Alison, who with her master's degree and sunny outlook on life, would seem destined for success. The absolute opposite was true. When she initially took *Organize Your Life*, the course, she was about to lose her apartment, was unemployed, and her health wasn't great. She felt utterly and completely stuck. In the discussion of the value of time, Alison realized that she was not placing any degree of importance on her time, and thus, neither was anyone else.

I taught Alison and her fellow students that all time has value. When we assign a numerical value to our time, even if this is a projection of our desire, our world begins to shift. We change our decisions, perhaps not spending an hour on the phone with someone who is complaining or making a decision whether to watch two hours of 'must-see' TV. Allocating a dollar amount to our time changes our perspective. The difference between the world's millionaires and billionaires and those that struggle financially is that they have a greater appreciation of the value of their time.

Consider this – a millionaire, working forty hours per week, has a time valued at $500 per hour. Someone making $10,000,000 per year has a time value of $5000 per hour. A billionaire has a time value of $500,000 per hour. If your time was worth $500,000 per hour, do you think you would waste it watching every kitten video on YouTube™? Of course not.

I shared with Alison that we want to value our time as a millionaire would before we actually get there. In doing this, we fully understand that every wasted minute is costing us $8.33! Therefore, if we spend fifteen minutes on the phone with a person who wants to share the latest gossip, it just cost us $125! I highly doubt that Warren Buffet, who made $25,694 per minute in 2013, wasted time during his production hours, tooling around Facebook or looking for games to play.

The bottom line is this – we teach the world how to treat us, and if you are feeling that people take advantage of you, then stop blaming the people and start looking in the mirror. Your time may be worth $8.33 an hour right now; however, the moment you start managing yourself in time like the millionaires and billionaires of the world, you just might become one.

Analyze Your Day

How often do we go through our days on 'autopilot?' We get up, we go through the motions of our lives, and at the end of the day, we end up feeling exhausted and overwhelmed, as though we didn't accomplish anything. One of the greatest personal development exercises we can ever do is to write down everything we do in a day.

Consider that we all have the same twenty-four hours; it is what we do with them, or specifically what we choose not to do with them, that creates the results we achieve. To truly create more balance, productivity and results in our lives, we must be willing to go under the microscope and analyze our activities. Are we doing the things that produce the outcomes we desire, or are we wasting time? In the following exercise, we will take a look at how you spend your day so that you can identify where you are not being as deliberate as you could be.

Step One – Write It Out

Stop reading right here and write down everything you did yesterday. Include things such as brushing your teeth, making the bed, having breakfast, social media, details about what you did with work, etc. It does not have to be chronological—just get it down on paper.

Step Two - Assign a Value

There are three types of actions we take in a day:

1. Those that move us toward our dreams.
2. Those that take us away from our dreams.
3. Those that allow us to dream.

Beside each activity write '1, 2 or 3.' Take a good look at what you have down. Is there a predominant number? You may be saying, 'Susan, I changed diapers yesterday – how is that a 1,2 or 3?' The truth is that at some point you dreamed of having this child even if it wasn't planned. By changing diapers, you are living into your dream of raising a healthy, strong individual. Eating healthy food, as an example, takes us toward our dream of living into a fit, lean body. Eating junk food, on the other hand, takes us away from that dream. As you go through this exercise, something I want you to truly grasp is this – people who are successful do very few things that take them away from the life they want to create.

Take a look at your numbers – I mean really take a look. Are you wasting time? Are you doing things that sabotage your success? If this is the case, then understand that you have the power to change; you have the inherent ability to shift what you do in your day, and I want you to start right now.

The Dream Building Essential Five

Look at your day and ask yourself this question – 'If I were to live this day again, and feel happier and more fulfilled, what five things would I not repeat?' Perhaps you spent too much time worrying or wasted precious minutes trying to find your car keys or glasses. Maybe you had a fight with your partner or cut someone off in traffic. Possibly you ate something you knew didn't serve your health. Whatever it was, we all do things that we wouldn't want to repeat.

5 Dream Stealing Activities

1.

2.

3.

4.

5.

Now that you see this list of five, and conceivably, you are tempted to write more than five, make a decision to not repeat these behaviors. These things are time wasters and not just in the moment; if something is pulling us away from our dreams, we must appreciate the old adage – two steps forward, one step back. One thing done that moved us back is not necessarily neutralized by one thing that moved us forward.

Lets take, for example, someone who decides to eat a pint of ice cream, which is over a thousand calories. That person would have to invest extra time in exercising to deal with the excess calories. The average weight individual burns a mere six hundred calories by running for an hour. In base terms, even someone who gets up and runs it off would have to run for over an hour and a half, much more than the average person can manage.

As an aside, I was a distance athlete for years, and I thought that because I was training so hard, I could eat whatever I wanted. Interestingly enough, the more I ate, the more weight I gained–go figure! Just because I was training and moving toward my dreams of podium finishes didn't mean that I could eat pints of ice cream. For me, it wasn't just about the calories – it was about an allergy to dairy that left me feeling sluggish, tired, and with severe digestive upset. That ice cream, although a sweet reward, took me away from my dreams because I would feel awful for the next two days, thus costing me valuable training time and just putting me in a bad mood, period.

To undo the 'ice cream' effect, I would obviously have to abstain from dairy for days, shorten my workouts, drink extra water, take additional enzymes and get more sleep. While these are all good dream building activities, I had to do several things just to neutralize the damage done by one pint of ice cream – Ben and Jerry's Chunky Monkey to be precise. It wasn't until I took a good, hard look at what I wanted in life (to be a professional triathlete at the time) and the ways in which I was self-sabotaging, that I stopped with the behaviors that held me back. Eventually, I did hit those podiums before being diagnosed with MS, and those memories are not worth all the ice cream in the world.

When we fully realize that time is finite, then we understand that any second spent on something that pulls us away from what we desire is a second that could conversely be spent on something that brings us closer to what we want. Just as doing something that takes us away from our dreams may require two or more actions to neutralize the effect, doing something that moves us toward our dreams may require two or more dream depleting activities to even make a dent.

Next, write down the five essential things that you know bring you closer to your dreams, whether you did them yesterday or not. For example, if I am in sales, then making connections with potential clients is an essential activity. Exercise is something that is essential to all of us; it brings us closer to a healthy, balanced life – it is definitely one of these five. Spending quality time with our loved ones may also be on your essential list. Getting seven hours of quality sleep may also be there. These five essential things will start to make up the foundation of your day, so choose wisely.

5 Essential Dream Building Activities

1.

2.

3.

4.

5.

Now that you have this list, ask yourself where you can replace the time spent on dream stealing activities with dream building activities. What if, for example, you stopped prowling around on Facebook and actually made prospecting calls? What if you chose to give up TV during the week and instead spent that time working out? Success is merely about how we choose to spend our time, and always remember that anyone who has something you want is spending their time in different ways than you do.

I worked with a couple that desperately wanted to change their lives. They started a business outside of their full-time jobs where they were working fifty to sixty hours per week. They made a commitment to contact three potential clients every single day, Monday thru Friday, no matter how tired they were. This was an essential activity that took them closer to their dreams. Within one year, they were able to let go of one of their jobs, and after the second year, they went into semi-retirement with their business, never having to report to a boss again.

Imagine for a moment that this couple allowed themselves to focus on other areas that didn't produce results – what would have happened then? By making a commitment that connecting with prospects was an essential activity, they inherently declared that other things, such as watching television or surfing the Web, were not important. This activity moved them toward their dreams, and with that level of consistency, they were able to take one day off every week and fully unplug from business and work. This allowed them to dream and re-charge.

If they can do it, so can you. You can truly live into optimal health, more fulfilling relationships and a stronger financial fortress by making better choices. Change often takes time to sink in, and at first, it may be tempting to reach for the pint of ice cream after the kids have gone to bed or drink the bottle of wine instead of going to the gym; however, as you eventually live into more dream building activities, you will become addicted to better results, and those dream stealing activities of the past will slowly fade from memory.

Organize Your Life

1. Decide how much your time is worth.

2. Analyze your day – write it out.

3. Assign value to each activity.

4. What are your non-essential five?

5. What are your essential five?

Chapter Four
The Art of Saying 'No.'

"To succeed in life, you need two things: ignorance and confidence."

-Mark Twain

Say 'No' to the Good

I once heard my fellow co-author, Jack Canfield, say, *"If you want to be successful, you will have to learn how to say 'no' to the good so you can say 'yes' to the great."* That really triggered some deep, palpable emotions for me as I realized I was saying 'yes' to a great many things for reasons that were not necessarily empowering to my circumstances. Saying 'no' can be daunting; we want to please people, we feel as though we are letting others down, or perhaps we fear that people will not like us if we start saying 'no.'

The word 'no' often triggers a host of emotions. We recall being denied as a child or the rejection that came when we made a sales call. The word 'no' is something that the wealthiest, most successful people on the planet use on a daily basis, and if we want to be successful, then saying 'no' must become a part of our regular vocabulary. The wealthy understand that 'no' is not often personal; it is merely a matter of a quick assessment – will saying 'yes' to this get me closer to my goal? If not, the answer is 'no.'

People who struggle in life tend to say 'yes' to the wrong things. They say 'yes' to must-see TV when they fully understand that their family is feeling neglected. They say 'yes' to, 'Do you want a second, or third, helping?' when they know they have weight to release. They say 'yes' to, 'Let's go out for drinks tonight,' instead of doing the sales calls they know they should make. Your life right now is a result of what you have chosen to say 'yes' and 'no' to. If you want a different result, then it is time to start saying, 'no' in a graceful, tactful and deliberate way.

In the previous chapter we discussed the questions:

- *Does this move me closer to my dreams?*
- *Does this take me further away from my dreams?*
- *Does this allow me to dream?*

If you want an easy way to assess saying 'no' to something, then ask the same questions.

I am often asked for my time for a variety of reasons. I used to say 'yes' to every request because of my perceptions that I would let people down if I wasn't always available. What ultimately happened was that I ended up resenting all of the commitments I had made; at the heart of the matter, I was disappointed in myself for saying 'yes' to so much. When I truly began to value my time and stepped back to take a moment to ask myself the key questions from the previous chapter, things began to shift. Today, I do say 'no,' and although it sometimes feels a little bit challenging, at the end of the day, I understand that my time is finite. I create space to do more of the things that take me toward my dreams by saying 'no' to those things that are only so-so.

The more successful you become, the more people will ask you for time, money and all sorts of things. You may be struggling financially right now, but that is a reflection of what you have chosen to say 'yes' to, and by no means is that an excuse to not say 'no.' If something does not take you toward your dreams or allow you to dream, then 'no' is perfectly fine. For example, let's say a friend has a 'make money quick scheme,' and you realize in your heart that it doesn't feel right. Although the allure of up front money may be tempting, you would only be saying 'yes' for the wrong reasons. You might feel that perhaps you would be letting down your friend if you do not get involved, or there might be the seduction of quick money without really giving thought to how your short-term actions may affect your overall life.

Saying 'no' requires being bold, assertive and trusting your gut. It also illustrates an individual who is clear on their goals, values their time, and is happily setting boundaries. Furthermore, 'no' for now does not mean 'no' forever, and in this chapter, we will learn the art of saying 'no' and how to graciously create boundaries that will free us up to do more of the things that shape the life we want to live.

What Can You Graciously Uncommit To?

I met a woman once who was grossly overcommitted. She helmed a massive family business, sat on three boards, had started two other companies, made appearances at every major social event around the globe, spent massive amounts of time seeking out only au currant fashions from this season, and was in the process of renovating a house. Her adrenals were fatigued, she was gaining weight, forgetting things, and of course, had lost her zest. I asked her what she could let go of, and she looked at me blankly, "I just don't know," she replied, "I just don't know."

She knew she needed to do something but didn't know where to begin. She wanted to hire me to do some consulting on her life – where I literally look at everything you do and help you simplify, but she was too 'busy' to take the time. What I would have done with her was to first have her clearly define her life goals in the areas of health, relationships and money. Then she would be asked to make a list of everything she was doing, and then ask her to rate, using the 1,2,3 system, which things were actually moving her forward and those things that were taking her away from where she wanted to be.

From this point, we would go through those items that did not enforce her goals and have her graciously uncommit. One of this woman's goals was to find her perfect partner. She met many men at all of these functions, but the relationships were challenging. After all – where would she ever have time? Another goal was to get healthy, but going from party to party, meeting to meeting and function to function meant many meals out, alcohol and late nights. How could these things work together? They didn't. You see, if our goals are not in alignment with our actions, we will never get what we want.

What this woman required was space – space to be healthy and space to have time with her future love. Her schedule was non-stop ten months out of the year. She took two months to de-compress; however, lasting health and a hot, passionate relationship are not things that we can only spend two months doing. Both of these things require daily time. In her life, it would be essential to free up space every day to exercise and have time to be with her new love. This would mean letting go of some of the things she had committed to.

For many achievers, filling a calendar is not a problem. We can do it quite easily. The tough part is backing out of commitments when we have already given our word. This all comes down to choices, and the first step is to identify those things we truly want to back out of by asking ourselves the following question– if I could graciously back out of any obligation, and no one would be upset, what would I choose? In the case of this woman, there were several items that she listed. If I were coaching her, I would have her identify five over the coming year. Immediately, this would shift her time commitment, offering her space to live into her current goals.

Graciously uncommiting is simple. I have done it time and again in my life, and guess what? The world didn't end. People who genuinely wanted to do business with me continued to do business with me, and ultimately, I ended up feeling better. Here are five ways you can graciously uncommit:

1. **Find a Replacement** – *'Bob, you know how I said I would help out on the fund raising committee. I am working on a new project that is taking much more time than I anticipated. The amount of time I have to commit right now is negligible. I do not want to leave you in a bind and have found a suitable candidate for my replacement.'*

2. **Improve the Atmosphere** – *'Sharon, I know your party is going to be a huge success. You are such a great hostess. When I initially accepted, I had a lot of energy. Right now, with so many things going on, my energy is not where it usually is. I wouldn't want to be the 'wet blanket' at your soiree, so please excuse me this time. Would you include me next time?'* You can send flowers instead.

3. **If I – Would You?** – *'Julie, women like us are always on the go. There is no end of things on our 'to-do' list. Listen, something landed in my lap, and it is demanding my attention this week. If I took the next two weeks of carpooling, would you take this week?'*

4. **Matching Mission** – *'Eric, your charity sounds amazing. I think the work you are doing is going to be wildly successful with the right group of like-minded people. Unfortunately, after careful deliberation, this does not match my charitable mission. Should you expand in this area, would you please re-visit me?'*

5. **Win-Win Solution** – *'James, you know how I promised to come in early and stay late for the next two weeks while we finish the project? I have thought of a win-win solution. It takes me an hour and a half to commute each*

day which totals almost one full workday every week. What if I log-on and work from home one day per week, so I can add those extra unusable hours. Perhaps we can nail this and make it even better than we had planned.'

A Second Level of Certainty - Trust Your Gut

According to neuroscientists, and validated by articles such as, *Think Twice: How the Gut's Second Brain Influences Mood and Well-Being,* published in *Scientific American,* our gut has millions of neurons, the same specialized cells that are found in our brain. Connectivity between the gut and the brain makes sense anatomically; however, scientists are still unraveling the mysteries of how this 'second brain' may influence our day-to-day life.

Have you ever committed to something only to feel sick to your stomach? Have you ever had a conversation that turned in a direction that caused you to feel anxious or unsure? This happens to all of us, and what I teach my students is to trust their guts. If you are trying to decide on whether to do something or not, visualize yourself doing and see how it makes you feel.

I once committed to do a speaking event for about two thousand people. After doing my initial questions, it became clear that, yes, this event would help to get me closer to my goals. It made sense to our team as well, and we did all of the usual things that we do to prepare – booking travel, planning the talk, social media promotion and arranging my schedule to accommodate my absence. Although it was business as usual, every time I thought of the event I felt a little uneasy. I remained committed because that was my word.

As the event approached, I started waking up during the night. Generally, I am a great sleeper, so this was cause for concern. Merely planning my talk or preparing the slides made me uneasy. Having done several events for audiences of 10,000 plus, I was very familiar with healthy anticipation versus anxiety, and there was nothing healthy about this feeling.

The day before I was scheduled to leave I woke up feeling ill. I was nauseous; I felt as though I was going to vomit. Every time I thought about the event, I got sicker and sicker. Chris came into my office and said, "Why don't you cancel?" The thought of going against my word felt slightly crippling; however, the thought of not doing the event immediately, and I want to emphasize that word, caused me to feel lighter. I knew what I had to do. The moment I canceled I felt better, and other things in my life started to fall into place.

In the end, everything was for the better. The day before I canceled we received an email letting us know that our son would be acknowledged at the sports banquet at his new school. This was no small event because prior to that year, our son, who is on the Aspherger's spectrum, never played team sports, was bullied in school and generally had great apprehension when it came to social activities. At his new school, he had played on the flag football, basketball and soccer teams all in one year. By not going to the speaking event, I would be able to attend his awards banquet.

The day I was supposed to fly, my friend, a *NY Times*™ best-selling author, called me with two great ideas. I also was able to spend some much needed time writing this book. In the end, having this extra time at home was a tremendous gift, one that occurred because I trusted my gut.

Do you have upcoming commitments that are causing you to feel uneasy? Is there something in your schedule that doesn't feel right? Inherently, we are all beautifully created by the Divine, and our gut instinct is there to guide us. The bottom line is that if your gut is telling you that something should be re-scheduled, canceled or avoided, then learn to trust. Part of living a balanced life is being in harmony with your body.

Pushing through when you feel that something is off is a sure fire way to take yourself out of balance.

You Are Committed – Make the Best of It

You might be thinking, 'Susan, this is great, but I have something that I absolutely cannot back out of. I do not really want to do it; however, my word is my word.' I get it. We have all been there, and it happens. There is a saying I use in mentoring business people – *"You do not have to be the island."* Essentially, by trying to do everything yourself, you are likely going to be consistently ineffective with the end result being exhaustion and overwhelm.

If you are committed to something and it isn't feeling quite right, ask yourself how you can make the best of the situation. Is there a benefit that you haven't quite taken the time to explore? Is there someone who can assist you with the task? Can you ask your family or your partner to help you create some space so you can focus? There are always ways to make the best of a situation if we take the time to figure it out.

Over the years, I have helped organize many events. For a long time, I ran a program based on my book – *The Have It All Woman*. Over three days, we helped women create a solid foundation in the core areas of their lives. It was beautiful and powerful to see women transform before our eyes. In the beginning, we ran the event with three people. The end result was that we were all exhausted for weeks afterward. The next event we added some volunteers, and instead of extreme fatigue at the end of the weekend, we all felt energized. As the saying goes, *"Many hands make light work."*

Whether you have a project to complete, an event to run, fundraising to do, or whatever it is, even a second opinion can be valuable. Seek out someone who has done what you are doing before (Google and YouTube are phenomenal sources, too) and get fresh perspective. Perhaps there are ways to make the project more streamlined or have a better result with less effort. Ultimately, you do not want to be the island, and whenever possible, always lighten the load.

Going Against Your Nature

Oprah Winfrey once said, *"It is better to be respected than to be liked."* If you are a 'yes-a-holic,' someone who says yes to everyone like Helen-Helps-A-Lot, then you will feel that saying 'no' and uncommitting goes against your nature. There might be a tremendous initial sense of guilt. The word guilt comes from the old English word 'gylt.' The meaning was sin, crime or moral defect. In today's world, the meaning is much more generalized, and we tend to use it lavishly to convey a wide range of emotion. Men and women feel guilty for not spending enough time with their kids. We teach children to feel guilty about not getting along, contributing or even having stress. We are indeed a guilt ridden generation.

The reality is that it is not a crime to say 'no.' You are no less of a person for maintaining a priority. If someone is going to sacrifice their friendship, or business relationship with you, just because you said 'no,' then they were not truly a loyal partner to begin with. Saying 'no' at times is not a selfish thing; in fact, it can be the most selfless thing you do. What good are you if you are spread thin, overwhelmed and exhausted, just going through the motions of life?

To truly Step Into Your Power™, you must embrace 'no,' so that when you do say 'yes,' it stems from a place of love, an origin of wanting to sincerely do something. You are not less of a person for saying 'no.' What you are is someone who is on their way to designing a life of integrity and meaning. Be strong. Stay focused and embrace your inner wisdom – it will guide you.

Organize Your Life Now

1. Look at the past few weeks. Where did you say 'yes' to something that took you further away from your dreams?

2. Look at your schedule for the coming weeks and months. Where can you graciously uncommit to five things?

3. If you have something that you have committed to and cannot shift the plans, see where you can negotiate to take the burden off.

4. Trust your gut. If something doesn't feel right – make a decision to back out.

5. Embrace the word 'no.'

Chapter Five
Creating a Schedule That Works for You

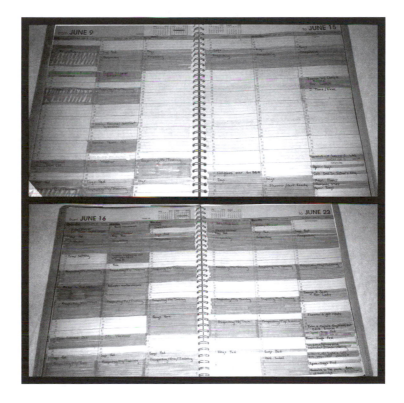

"If you do what is hard, your life will be easy.
If you do what is easy, your life will be hard."

-T. Harv Eker

It's Your Life

You may or may not remember the catchy Bon Jovi song entitled, *It's My Life.* It became an anthem for the turn of the millennium, one that signified a monumental time in history. The following lyrics, derived from the chorus are a pointed reminder that we always want to remember that, yes, this is indeed our life and no one else's.

I've asked myself

How much do you

Commit yourself?

It's my life

Don't you forget

It's my life

It never ends

When it comes to creating a schedule, the first and foremost rule is that this is YOUR life, comparing yourself to anyone else is only going to serve to take you out of balance. People often come up to me and say, 'I don't know how you do it,' or 'I could never do what you do.' Either way, it is irrelevant because we lead different lives. Yes, I use ALL of the techniques outlined in this book to create a life of productivity, fulfillment and balance.

Although the proficiencies are universal for the most part, the demands of our lives are very likely entirely different.

I often read *Harper's Bazaar* magazine. My favorite section is '24 Hours With...' In this particular feature, celebrities and designers are asked to chronicle what they do in a 24 hour period. I find this fascinating as I observe the habits of some of the most well-known people on the planet. Looking at how much someone sleeps, what they eat, how they produce and what they do to unplug is a wonderful exercise in sociology, one that also lends valuable insight into how the uber wealthy live their lives.

An observation that I have made in reading these '24 Hours With' pieces is that highly successful people are very disciplined and ritualistic. Many of them will wake at the same time every day, eat their meals at the same time, produce in their businesses at the same time and follow individual rituals. They also tend to work longer hours and appear to feel an intense commitment to their enterprise.

Having a healthy curiosity about someone else's schedule is an extremely positive approach to first contemplating your own schedule. Conversely, being jealous of someone else's results will only serve to take us away from our goals. We can learn a great deal from observing those who have achieved success in an area of life we desire. If you know someone who has accomplished a goal that is on your list, then ask them how they spend their day. What do they make a priority? How do they quantify their results? What do they read? How do they schedule their time? We will never learn anything by jealousy; we will learn everything by curiosity.

What the Rich Do That the Poor Do Not

Thomas Corley, author of *Rich Habits: The Daily Success Habits of Wealthy Individuals,* followed wealthy people—defined by those earning over $160,000 per year and having a net worth of at least $3.2 million, and conversely, those considered not well-off – having an annual income of $35,000 or less and a liquid net worth of $5,000 or less. The following are five of Corley's observations of the habits the rich have that the poor do not:

1. **Rich people always keep their goals in sight.** Corley found that the wealthy agree with this sentiment 62% of the time, whereas the poor agree only 6% of the time. 67% of the wealthy put their goals in writing every day.

2. **Rich people know what needs to be done today.** 81% of the wealthy had a daily task list, whereas only 19% of the poor did. Corley found that 67% of the rich complete 70% or more of their daily tasks.

3. **Rich people do not watch television.** 67% of the wealthy watched one hour or less of television daily. 77% of poor people watched one hour or more. 6% of rich people watch reality television, whereas 78% of the poor do.

4. **Rich people love reading.** 86% of the wealthy love to read, and 88% of them read for self-improvement for 30 minutes each day. Only 2% of the poor had the same habit.

5. **Rich people give more than expected at work.** 81% of the wealthy, compared to 17% of the poor, said that they give more than expected at work. 86% of rich people spend over 50 hours per week working while only 43% of the poor did.

Essential and Non-Essential

In our day, we have several things that are essential – sleeping, bathing, exercising, generating income, and perhaps we have children or adult family members living with us that are reliant upon us to a degree. Within these areas, there are sub-areas – for example, if you have a business, then perhaps social media is an essential activity. If you have children, you may have to take them to and from school and also to lessons, practice, or other activities.

In the previous chapter, Managing Ourselves in Time, we looked at our essential five and non-essential five dream building activities. From this vantage point, we can now begin to create a schedule that works for OUR life. My observation has been that the wealthy have disciplined schedules, and those that struggle financially do not – they ebb and flow as the wind blows, so to speak, and are what some would refer to as 'all over the map.' Whatever your objectives are, you've got to have a schedule. Period! I teach my students that if it isn't written down – it isn't happening.

My students are taught to schedule everything...yes, I mean absolutely everything. From date nights with their partner to individual time with kids, production time, admin, and even time to dream – it is all written down in a paper day planner. We will get to that in a moment. Planning is the key to success, and the better our schedule is laid out, the more likely we are to create results.

Make a list of all of the essential things you do in a week. Beside each item, allocate an amount of time. The majority of people underestimate the amount of time it takes to do something, so add an extra ten minutes to each activity to be on the safe side. Be sure to also include commuting time to and from each activity.

Here is a list to get you started and you may have more.

- Sleeping
- Bathing
- Personal Hygiene
- Health Care Visit
- Eating
- Exercising
- Making Love to Your Partner
- Looking for a Partner
- Working
- Business Correspondence
- Social Media and Marketing

- Going to Your House of Worship
- Prayer/Meditation
- Banking
- Cleaning the House
- Taking Children to School and Programs
- Taking Children to the Doctor or Dentist
- Doing Homework with Children
- Paying Bills
- Laundry
- Cooking
- Home Repairs
- Landscaping

Once you have your list and have allocated the amount of time it takes to do each thing weekly, then ask yourself – 'Where can I delegate or delete five of these items to free up more time?' We all do things that are not essential to daily life. When we can hire someone to do something or delegate it to a family member, we open up our schedule, so we can do more of the things we love.

Cleaning the Toilet While Doing Business Calls

Many years ago, I reached a tipping point. I had started a business from my home, and it was generating about $250,000 per year in income. I found myself with my headset on, doing a call while cleaning a toilet. I thought, 'This is insane.' I knew I needed to hire a housekeeper; however, my husband and I had argued over this point. He thought it was a waste of money while I, on the other hand, was doing a large amount of the cleaning. He had not grown up with a housekeeper; his mother did the bulk of the work.

Even though my husband respected me as a businesswoman, he lived in fear of spending the money. We often fought about this point, and it was causing a tremendous amount of stress and resentment. Something had to change. One day I calmly said this, "I have been looking into getting a housekeeper. It will cost us about $100 per week. If I make an extra hundred dollars each week, can we get one?" It wasn't really a request, but by using the 'if I...would you,' technique, he was much more open. That year was 2005, and we have had someone cleaning our house ever since.

Yes, you may have to have some tough conversations and agree to compromise. In the end, it will absolutely be worth it.

I completely understand that you might have children at home who haven't lifted a finger or a partner who was raised in a certain way. Let people know lovingly that things are about to change, and although it may be uncomfortable for a time, everyone will eventually benefit.

Five Hours Per Week for Your Monkey

The first thing we want to look at is this – is that monkey still on your back? Many of my students have a tax monkey, meaning they haven't filed in over a year or they are overwhelmed with paper. Your monkey could come in many forms. Perhaps you urgently need to generate extra income, or you have a health concern going on. Whatever that monkey is, it is going to howl, shriek, and jump up and down to get attention. The monkey is always the first thing we block off time for in the week regardless of how much you don't want to deal with it.

I had a student who hadn't filed taxes in several years. She was overwhelmed with paper and frankly, thought she could just 'fly under the radar' and not deal with it. Having taken my class, she knew this was a big monkey. She was also fully aware, from the lessons, that any monkey not dealt with was tying up emotional and physical energy. With her schedule, I coached her to dedicate time to dealing with this particular monkey. Fortunately, her children were grown, and she was working part-time, so finding suitable hours was not a challenge.

She set aside five hours each week to deal with the monkey. Within five weeks (seriously – ironic, I know), she had fully dealt with the taxes and found out that she was getting a small refund. After that, things in her life changed. Whether related or not, a relationship with one of her children that had been strained, miraculously healed. This lady had more energy and decided to take a class. With renewed freedom, she also made a massive decision to sell her home and relocate across the country to start a new life. I fully believe that if she hadn't dealt with the monkey, she would have remained stuck.

Schedule Everyone In

I once read that Madonna scheduled individual dates with her four children. Some bloggers were aghast. What good mother would do that? My response is this – what good mother wouldn't? It may sound contrived to schedule dates with your children or your spouse; however, I guarantee that unless something is scheduled, it is a slippery slope as to whether that date happens or not. Pretty soon, weeks go by and you wonder when the last time you had a quality moment with your loves was.

In our house, date night is absolute. It is Thursday night. Chris and I either go out or stay in. No matter what, we shut down our computers and mobile devices by six o'clock. If I am traveling or speaking at an event, then we move our date night. Knowing that we have this time to look forward to provides incredible infrastructure to our relationship. We also schedule in time to be intimate.

Pause. Yes, you heard that right. We schedule it in. You may be saying, 'That is crazy. Where is the spontaneity?' The answer is that, for us, once you factor in kids, running multiple companies, and life, if we didn't schedule it, it wouldn't happen as often. A 2014 article in the Huffington Post asked married couples how often they have sex. The answer varied across the board; however, many couples decrease their amorous encounters with age and the onset of children.

Studies show that the more sex we have, the more we want. Furthermore, the less sex we have, the less sex we want. It is the proverbial double-edged sword. It may not be overly romantic to schedule it in, but won't it be more likely to happen if there is time? Of course.

I had a friend who hadn't had sex with his wife in four years. Sadly, they had become more like friends than lovers. At the advice of his therapist, he and his wife made a decision to schedule it in. Their time was Sunday mornings when the children were at a program. At first, it felt contrived, but eventually they got into a routine and had fun with it. Just by doing it once, they had had more sex in one day than they had in four years. Something to think about.

If you do not have a partner, you want to schedule in time to find your ideal partner. In other words – if you are single, get out there and mingle if it is something that is important to you. I had a friend who was widowed at a young age and became a single mom. After a few years, she decided that she was ready to share her life again. One night a week she hired a babysitter and went to a meet-up group. Within a year, she found a wonderful man, and they got married.

Whether it is your partner, potential partner, your child, or someone you care about, schedule everyone in. From family times to date nights, the people in your life will appreciate that you have carved out time just for them.

Money Matters

Whether you have a job or own a business, we generally require time to make and manage our money. I have retirees who take my class and I have millennials. Even those with assets over a million dollars should schedule time weekly to manage their money. In the chapter on organizing our finances, we will discuss more about this topic, but for the time being, you are in one of a few places:

1. You need to create more income.

2. You are generating income, but it is flowing out equally as fast.

3. You have solid income, are financially stable and in a place that you can simply manage your money.

Whatever we put our attention on, we get. If we need more income, then we must schedule in time to create it. That may be having a home-based business or perhaps actively seeking a new, or better, job. Either way, if we schedule time to generate cash flow, it is much more likely to happen.

The same is true of wealth management. Having money to actively manage and being able to generate more money from our existing reserves is a good place to be. Having made and lost money, I will tell you from first-hand experience that it only took one time of not actively presiding over my income and losing it all to teach me the valuable lesson that money management must be a priority.

Every week, you want to schedule in time to go into your online banking and review the transactions. I choose to do this daily; however, you may not have as many line items flowing through. Furthermore, I take time once each week to look at my portfolio and actively work with my trader to see what we want to do. Because I put my attention on both wealth creation and wealth management, my income and my assets increase year to year. If you schedule these things in, I have no doubt that your circumstances can and will improve.

Time to Unplug

How connected are we? With our devices, we can literally be plugged-in to someone or something 24/7. The question is – how healthy is it to be so constantly available? In Tim Ferriss' bestselling book, *The 4 Hour Work Week*, he espoused the virtues of unplugging an hour before bed and reading, yes reading...fiction! His premise was that it takes our brains time to shut down and prepare for a restful sleep. For my students, and for Chris and I, this is non-negotiable.

The other thing we schedule in is one unplug day per week. In our family, this is Sunday. I shut down my cell phone late Saturday afternoon and do not turn it on until Monday morning. I do not answer texts, emails or actively go on social media. Exceptions would be if I am traveling or, as was the case in 2015, when we attended the Super Bowl and our team won. We definitely posted updates.

Our family loves Sundays. We are much more relaxed, and this time is wonderful to recharge. Chris and I often go running, and then we head to church. We spend the afternoon playing, swimming or even napping. At night, we sit down for dinner and then perhaps watch a movie. By Monday morning, I am ready to go, fully rested and refreshed. Interestingly enough, when we started doing this, our income increased dramatically.

I read that entrepreneur, Ivanka Trump, and her husband, Jared Kushner, honor the Sabbath and shut down their cell phones from Friday at sundown until Saturday at sundown. Trump, who converted to Judaism, reportedly finds this time rejuvenating;

she focuses on family, unwinding and recharging. Both she and her husband are multi-millionaires.

Schedule in one day a week or, at the very least, twenty-four hours to fully unplug. You will feel much more energized as you head into the next six days. My students do this, and they have found their stress lowers, mood improves, and they have much more focus and drive to put towards all aspects of their life.

Write It Down

My friend and mentor, Sandy Botkin, a former IRS attorney and CPA, suggests that entrepreneurs write down everything they do, as eventually they may be audited. I teach my students to keep an old-fashioned paper day planner. I personally like the Day Minder which showcases the entire week at a glance. It is available from Staples™ and Office Max™ and www.ataglance. com.

The paper planner is an excellent back-up. Although I do also use an online calendaring system, occasionally in business the following have happened to me, and I have no doubt that they could happen to you:

- My computer has crashed.
- Prolonged power outage.
- Identity theft that forced password changes.
- Computer virus which prevented me from logging on until it was remedied.
- Audit.

The reason I love a paper planner is that it is an absolute. If your computer goes down or your mobile device crashes, then guess what? Your life continues on. Furthermore, if you are audited, a paper planner can validate your activities to reinforce your tax status. Sandy Botkin counsels that having everything stored to a Cloud is excellent and that having things written down is a double whammy.

When I lived in Canada, we had terrible storms. On more than one occasion, we lost power. One particular week our power went out for over twenty-four hours. Instead of missing a beat in business, I grabbed my paper planner and my cell and turned the car into an office.

At first, using a paper planner may seem archaic, but you will get used to it and even learn to embrace it. I also keep my planners because they can further validate past information such as travel and business meetings for the sake of taxes. When we moved to the United States, we had to make a list of all of our travel for the past several years. During that time, we had gone through several computers, and Clouds were not widely used. Thankfully, I had the paper planners, and all travel was neatly detailed within. Embrace the paper planner, especially if you are in business. It is essential to organizing your life.

Color-Coding Your Week

Take a moment and think about the core activities you have in a week:

- Spiritual and Physical Health
- Family/Friends
- Create and Manage Money
- Time to Dream
- Admin

Imagine a week that was well-balanced, where you felt empowered, energized and fulfilled – wouldn't that be incredible? Although you may feel that it sounds impossible, know that it is entirely feasible to live this way. What the average person does is fail to prepare. As the late Jim Rohn, one of my mentors and an exceptional business philosopher, used to say,

"Either you run the week or the week runs you." In other words, we have the power to determine what our week will look like, and this is what achievers do – they plan it in advance.

One of the techniques that works well for my students, and one that I employ as well, is to color-code my week. I assign a color to each activity and go through the planner, highlighting out the time. Anything that creates wealth is green. Family time, including groceries and other errands that support the home, is blue. Personal time is orange. Pink is time to dream and create. I use the time between these things as admin. I can be very efficient in returning emails and texts, so I choose to be flexible with that time.

We become extremely out of balance when our week takes a unilateral focus. For example, if you are working on a project at work and you get to the end of the week, you might become frustrated because you didn't work out, have quality time with your family, or catch up on other things. Your life will feel out of balance. Let's say, however, that you had the same demanding week, but you pre-planned and color-coded in time for a quick workout (more in the health chapter), time to read to your kids, and a thirty minute power 'date' with your partner; you would feel much more balanced because you would look at the past week knowing that you had at least done some things that you had wanted to do.

Benjamin Franklin once said, *"When we fail to plan, we are planning to fail."* When we do not plan our week in advance, we are setting ourselves up for potential feelings of lack of fulfillment and lack of accomplishment. Conversely, when we take the time to plan ahead, we are able to clearly delineate time compartments that will allow us to focus on what is important that week.

Get some highlighters and make a decision to define your week on your terms. If something is important, such as generating more income or dealing with a monkey, then highlight out the time to get it done. For the obsessed, myself included, you can color-code your online calendar in the same way and even assign colors to people so that when they email you, you know immediately what to respond to right away.

My students who run multiple businesses color-code their businesses separately. This helps them to maintain focus in various areas and remain highly productive. I do not recommend multiple calendars if you do have more than one venture. Everything should be centralized so that you do not miss anything. The best week has a rainbow of colors. Start by using this technique right away.

End It Before You Begin It

On several occasions, I had the opportunity to share the stage with Jim Rohn. He used to say, *"If you want to be successful, end your day before you start your day, end your week before you start your week, end your month before you start your month, and end your year before you start your year."* In other words, think clearly about how you want your time to be structured. The most productive people I know all have their lives laid out well in advance.

You may not currently be living the life of your dreams, but that should not stop you from taking control right now. The night before the upcoming day, take five minutes and plan out your activities. If you are in business, then schedule time to make sales and client calls. Another amazing mentor, *NY Times* Best Selling Author of *Swim With the Sharks or Get Eaten Alive*, Harvey Mackay, says, *"Do the things that make you the most money first."*

Each night before I go to bed, I review the coming day and list out the activities that I will be doing to generate revenue in my companies. If I have calls to make, then I pull the phone numbers and list them out in a notebook. If I know that I am going to be on a high-level call with a prospective business partner, I take extra time to Google them and look at their social media so I can be prepared.

On Sunday night, I plan out the entire week ahead. I see where the gaps are; have I scheduled adequate time to do those activities which are in alignment with my objectives for the week? For example, as I was writing this book, I sectioned off writing blocks and took Thursdays as full writing days. My team knew not to book appointments, and I even posted on social media that I was in writing mode most of the time. When I am working on a book project, writing an editorial, or creating content for my companies, time to be free of distractions is essential.

On Monday mornings, I meet with my team to review the week ahead. Things change, opportunities arise, and we have to be flexible. We also review how we can be more efficient and take into consideration the requests for time that have been tabled. In our review, we include my schedule, Chris' schedule, the social media schedule, pending requests and upcoming travel. On Fridays, the team meets separately for virtual training.

Our company is comprised of people working remotely along with contractors to fulfill various aspects. It is important that I am not the most important person in the meeting. For us, it is our customers and clients. We do our very best to work with everyone and also to ensure a balanced, flexible work environment. If someone wants to go to a playgroup or school musical during work hours – no sweat. We know that the time gets made up in other hours, which is perfectly fine, as we are operating with multiple time zones.

Chris and I also plan out meals for the week, so we are on task. We discuss who will be doing pick-ups, grocery shopping and even getting the money for our housekeeper. It isn't always perfect. We have missed our Sunday planning, and the greatest observation is that on the weeks where we have failed to plan, we have found ourselves feeling much less productive.

At the end of one month, we review the upcoming month using the same diagnostics. Are we being efficient? Are we committing to things that make sense? How can we improve? Asking ourselves these questions has helped us get better and better.

Once per year we meet face-to-face. We plan the coming year and assess our progress. The planning for the coming year is done in August or September. During this time, we look at our objectives, infrastructure, and share ideas. From this, we create a plan for the next year, which is essential to fall back on, especially for a small business.

Before the year ends, I take time create a personal plan for the coming year. I look at my relationship with God, health, relationships with Chris and the kids, charitable giving, finances, and all other aspects of my life. No year ever begins without me first envisioning exactly how I want it to be. I create a document, including photos, and have it coil-bound. During the year, I review it to see if I am on track. Generally speaking, 65% or more of what I write does come true. I fully believe that it is at least 50% more than if I did not take the time to do this.

Ultimately, we hear time and again that we get what we expect. If we go into our day, week, month and year with certain expectations, we are much more likely to achieve those desires of our heart than if we simply entered into each period of time with a lack of certainty. In this chapter, we covered how the rich create goals and daily objectives. This is not just a habit of those who create wealth; it is a habit of anyone who achieves anything. The faster you adopt this practice, the faster the results will manifest in your life.

Organize Your Life Now

1. It's Your Life – make a decision to avoid comparison when it comes to creating a schedule.

2. Schedule Time for the Monkey – five hours a week to get that monkey off your back.

3. Create a Balanced Schedule – time for wealth creation, health, family, friends and personal time.

4. Write It Down – if it isn't written down, it isn't happening...nor may you be able to validate that it actually did happen.

5. Plan Before You Start – write out your day in advance.

Chapter Six
Streamlining Communication

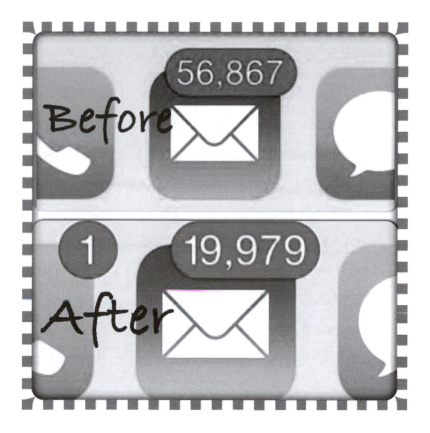

*"Successful people ask better questions,
and as a result, they get better answers."*

-Tony Robbins

You've Got Mail

Years ago, two actors, Meg Ryan and Tom Hanks, starred in a romantic comedy entitled, *You've Got Mail.* The year was 1998, and email was just becoming more mainstream. In one famous scene, Ryan's character eagerly awaits a message from Hanks in anticipation of receiving some form of delicious correspondence. Her email inbox was empty; the thrill of getting an email was palpable. My have things changed.

Sara Radicati, PhD, published a report on emails. The average person in business is expected to send and receive approximately 128 emails per day by the end of 2015, up from 89 in 2012. Globally, there are expected to be 4.1 billion email accounts by the end of 2015. Email is a staple of business. In our companies, Chris and I communicate with lawyers and accountants over email, not Facebook messaging or text. Email is likely to remain the primary method of communication for professionals for the next few years as long as maintaining communication trails is essential to validate our interactions.

The challenge for the disorganized person is that emails can build up. That person may tell themselves that they will get to the email, but the next day more emails pour in and the person becomes further behind. We then begin to send mixed messages - yes, we want to do business, or go on that date, or whatever it is, and yet, it isn't THAT important because we can't be bothered to respond.

Let me ask you a question - how many emails are in your inbox right now? Zero? One hundred or more? One thousand or more? Ten thousand or more? If you are sitting on hundreds or thousands of emails, why do you think that is? The likely answer is that, on some level, you are procrastinating on dealing with them. You tell yourself that you will get around to it, but the truth is that the likelihood is very slim.

You may be saying, 'So what Susan, these are just emails, it is not a big deal.' What I would like to propose, in my observation over time, is that your email inbox is a reflection of how you operate in life. The greater the number of emails, the more likely it is that you are a procrastinator. If you have kept emails that you rationalize you might need for business, but they sit there in the same general inbox as everything else, then you are also likely a person who isn't super organized in your finances either; anyone who can't file and deal with emails pertaining to money is not generally dealing with their finances effectively at all.

Deal With It

In my course, I have had several students with email inboxes in the tens of thousands. In this section, I will share with you the tips that I give them to deal with the chaos. Time and again, when my students get their inbox under control, they feel a massive burden lifting. Just like decluttering your home office or your closet, purging out your inbox is also essential. Know that if you have an exorbitant amount of emails, this process is going to take you several hours. That being said, it does not have to be done all at once, and when your inbox in under control, managing it can be done in five-minute blocks quite easily. Here are the steps:

1. **Create Essential Folders -** Depending on your life, not all of the following folders will be relevant. Choose which ones are essential to you.

   - **Business Receipts** - Often we receive electronic receipts. These are, of course, essential for tax purposes. When these come in, you have some options, and we will cover these in the chapter on money.

   - **Business Travel** - I travel often for business. For tax reasons, documented itineraries are essential to back-up deductions. Any emails that include flight receipts, hotel and rental car confirmations go in here.

- **Pending** - This file includes anything that is relevant to events within the next five weeks. These emails could include preparation for upcoming conference calls, webinars or meetings. Once the event has occurred, the email is either deleted from the file or placed elsewhere.

- **Family** - This folder is excellent for the photos someone sent you from the last reunion or any correspondence related to your children that you may need to keep, such as blood work from the doctor or confirmations of summer camp attendance. School correspondence may also go here.

- **Legal/Accounting** - Emails that contain contracts, correspondence from lawyers and accountants go here. Obviously, we want to have hard copies of these agreements that we store in a safe. Because Chris and I work together, we share documents, or I may need to have an agreement sent over to our C.O.O. or other team member; this way I have them at the ready.

- **Staff** - If you have a business and have emails pertaining to staff behavior, task management, etc., then create a separate folder for these communications.

- **Individual Companies** - Many of my students have more than one business. Each company may require a folder with appropriate subfolders. I store things such as conference call numbers, ongoing projects and events relevant to that company here.

2. **Start Sorting -** Depending on the number of emails in your inbox, sorting can be daunting. Here is how I suggest you do it:

- **'Key Word'** - Most email services have a keyword search. Type in 'receipt' as the first word, for example, and this should organize all emails related to receipts. Start filing these in business and family folders.

- **'From'** - It is very likely that not all of the senders in your email inbox are desirable. There could be spam or that person who sends you pages long emails that you no longer have a relationship with. Start deleting in the 'From' category. You will also want to sort in this category, too - for example, if you have five emails from your lawyer and none are urgent, then place them in the 'legal/accounting' file.

- **'Date Received'** - Sorting this way allows you to look at the chronology of the email. Sort oldest to newest. Simply holding down the 'delete' button or highlighting all of your old emails from 2010 and then purging them, although gratifying, is not suggested if you have a business. You could be deleting old business receipts that did not come up in your keyword search. Start deleting with caution.

- **'Flagging'** - As you go through, you may find emails that require attention. 'Flag' them so that, after you sort through, you can sort by 'flag' and get those things dealt with.

3. **Unsubscribe -** Companies want your email. The bigger the list, the better. In countries, such as Canada, there are strong anti-spam laws with large fines; however, companies get around this by using off-shore servers and routing ISP addresses. A great way to manage your emails is to use a service such as 'Unroll Me'. This will not work if you are on a private server, but it does do a great job if you are on a large platform like GMAIL™.

One cautionary tale is that you will potentially be unsubscribed from essential emails. My students, as an example, receive their homework and viewing link to the previous class in an email. When they 'unroll,' they often come back and say, 'I didn't get the homework.' Make sure you create a list of essential senders and re-enroll when you do this.

Lastly, if you have an old email address and that inbox if full of spam, then make your life easier and get a brand new email. You may have had the same email since you were fifteen; it is time to let it go and create a fresh start. There is something cathartic about a new beginning, and trust me, if people emailed you months, even years ago and haven't heard back yet, then they likely are not expecting to. Just press 'delete,' and embrace a new era of email happiness.

Short and Sweet Like a Tweet

I teach my students to streamline their communication by keeping emails, texts and any messages to one to three lines maximum. If we cannot keep it short, it requires a phone call. In my own life, when I receive an email that is pages long, it goes to a very low priority, unless it is some form of legal agreement, and believe me, these tend to be very long. Twitter™ became a sensation because it limited how much a person could say in their post; 140 characters max changed our worlds as, suddenly, our long drawn-out personal manifestos were not 'tweetable.'

Emails and other forms of messaging are not as constrained as Twitter™ though it would be helpful if they were. Sending long, verbose emails, unless they are for business and require such length, is just downright disrespectful. Consider the following for a person that makes a million dollars per year. Based on a forty-hour work week, their hourly wage is $500. If your email is over a page long and takes that person over fifteen minutes to read it, process it, and respond, you just cost them $125!

People do not need to know that the reason you are not producing in business is because you were bullied as a child, you cat vomited on your computer and that you have no money left in your bank account. Your backstory is not relevant and frankly, should never be put in an email. The reality is that the average person creates emails that are too lengthy and are a waste of other people's time.

A study at the University of Glasgow looked at the email habits of a U.K. based company called International Power. They found that executives spent 1.5 hours per day dealing with only 56 emails. In other words, instead of spending time generating revenue and actually doing business, they were tying up almost one entire workday per week with email. A simple recommendation was made - think twice before sending the email. This led to a staggering 10,000 plus hours saved per year by the company.

The bottom line is that it always starts with us. As we begin to communicate with brevity, others will follow suit. When an email is too long or requires a lengthy response, set up a time for a call. You can send a text saying, 'received your email - can you talk?' Chances are, if you are in business, that email is a big time drain on your day. Try limiting your emails to the same length as a tweet and observe how much more productive you become.

You Professional Signature

My students are taught to create email signatures that effectively communicate when they are available. Whether you have a business or not, having a professional email signature speaks volumes about you. In addition to a high resolution photo, I also recommend listing your website and hours of operation (for business owners). You will also want to have a business disclaimer, and I would encourage you to work with an attorney to develop one.

A great sample email signature may look like this:

Jill Makesalot

President and CEO

Makesalot Inc.

www.jillmakesalot.com

Office Hours

Monday thru Friday – 9:00 a.m. to 5:00 p.m. PST

(disclaimer)

I love the site www.emaildisclaimers.com. You can find great disclaimers there to use until you have one that fits your company.

Think Before You Type

A friend of mine, best-selling author, Sam Richter, suggests that people think before they type. It is easy to read an email or post and want to type a manifesto defending your position or reactively contradicting someone else's opinion; however, it is never healthy to respond in the heat of the moment. A great way to reign in your communication is to ask yourself if you would want your comments to be made public on the front page of the *NY Times.* If you have ever sent an email or posted something you later regretted, then you can fully appreciate that once something is 'out there,' it is tough to take back.

Many emails are forwarded. Furthermore, they can be kept for legal reasons. Let's say, for example, that you were really ticked off with a former business associate and 'let them have it' in an email. If that business associate tried to sue you for some reason, the email may support their claims against your character. A great rule is that if you are choosing to respond to this type of communication, set up a time for a phone conversation. If resolution doesn't seem possible, then acquire a neutral third party to mediate. The worst thing you can do is to put in writing any negative thoughts because these could also be copied and reposted for the entire world to see.

In my class, students are taught to keep any emails that are considered antagonistic and file them away in case they are needed. They are also taught to keep all correspondence upbeat and positive. One of my students, as an example, sought out advice on how to deal with a woman who had left her network marketing downline and attempted to cross-recruit some of her team. She was angry and frustrated. I suggested she simply message the woman and let her know that she wished her well and to gently remind her of her company's policies and procedures by saying something like this, 'If you have any questions about who you can and cannot bring with you, I suggest you refer to the policies and procedures.' She kept it to three lines, professional and warm.

Sometimes we have to be nice through gritted teeth. Yes, it is tough because people can be abusive, antagonistic and downright rude in their correspondence with us. By 'getting in the ring,' we lose valuable time because it is not just the minutes we spend crafting our response, but also the time we waste ruminating over it.

In life, there will always be people who disagree with your point of view or maybe even with you as a person. Let them have their opinion. I love what the late Eleanor Roosevelt said, *"No one can make you feel inferior without your consent."* By retorting back, attempting a written power struggle, we only serve to become highly distracted. When we are distracted, we are taken out of productivity and waste time. Think before you respond to an email or post. If you don't want the world to see it, then take a deep breath, go for a walk and move on.

The Five Minute Conversation

Whether we are responding to a lengthy email by electing to have a verbal conservation or dealing with someone who tends to be verbose, we can create boundaries for our conversations by telling the person beforehand how much time we have. Let's say someone has sent you a lengthy communique, and you want to respond. A great thing to do is to pick up the phone and say something like this, 'John, I just received your email, and I am in between appointments. I have five minutes right now - what can I assist you with?' If the person says, 'This will take more than five minutes,' and you know that it really won't, you can respond by saying, 'I am back-to-back today and really want to help you. Let's see what we can get accomplished.'

By choosing to be respectful of your own time, you also send a loud, clear message that your time is to be valued. People will often communicate with their own agenda; we all do it. The variable is that many people simply do not take into account the other factors in another person's life. For example, you might have children, and it is a holiday. Someone may want your time right now and maybe they do not have kids. If you choose to have the conversation, you can use the five minute rule and just deal with it. Then you will not be ruminating on it for the rest of the day.

This also applies to family members. Let's say you have a sister that has been complaining about her weight for the past two years. Every conversation is about how fat she feels. You love your sister, but her weight problem is making you feel heavy. When she calls, let her know you have five minutes. You can also use some of the other techniques in coming pages on clearing a path for better conversations.

Either way, we can all endure anything for five minutes. Love yourself enough to set some boundaries and feel really excited about it! Yes, some people may feel upset because you are no longer giving so much of your time. The truth is that you will feel so much better spending that extra time enjoying your family, investing in your career or getting that workout in. Furthermore, you will be amazed at how quickly people get to the point when they realize that they only have five minutes of your time.

Clearing the Way for More Efficient Communication

In business, time equals money. If you have a business, as many of my students do, you begin to appreciate those 12 five-minute blocks that comprise every hour. One of the things I do when

I begin to work with someone is to look at the areas in which they are wasting too much time in their communication. We then go on to look at how using some simple techniques can begin to streamline their efforts and increase their results.

The following three forms are used by my students. Some may be more applicable to you at this present moment; however, one never knows what can happen in the future. All of these strategies will begin to save you time.

1. **Request for Assistance Form -** Have you ever had someone email you, a team member, employee, colleague, or associate, with the title, 'help'? In the past, this used to happen to me often, and anytime I saw this, my cortisol (stress hormone) levels would rise. I love helping people. However, what would inherently happen was that I would get on a phone call with the person and the conversation would be draining; it was never just one problem – it was a series of things, and I ended up feeling more like a therapist than a business owner. When I worked corporately, employees would say, 'Hey, can I talk to you?' Because this was so nebulous, I ended up spending thirty minutes to an hour talking about problems and never making any headway. I realized that I was the common denominator; I

wanted to help people, but I did not want to spend an hour on the phone talking about a problem.

In my corporate days, I developed a modus operandi for my employees – if they had a problem, they had to come with three possible solutions. This began to streamline our time. When I went into business for myself, it finally clicked with inspiration from a friend. Why not have a form, which people would fill out prior to an appointment so that the time could best be spent on the solution. Thus, the 'Request for Assistance Form' was born.

When someone is requesting my time, they are sent this form. It allows me to help the person at a deeper level because I understand the nature of what we are going to talk about beforehand. The form has the following fields:

- Name
- Best Phone Number
- Best Email
- What do you want to accomplish in your time with Susan?
- If this is a challenge – what else have you tried?
- Who else has mentored you on this issue?

- Is there anything else you want to share? (140 characters max)

This form is emailed out, and the call is scheduled for 15 minutes. Because I value my time, the time is only offered to people who qualify – clients, customers, and business partners. The form must be submitted 24 hours before the call. Then, someone from my team will calendar it for me. This has saved me so much time and energy. The calls have become much more productive and solution based. I used to dread 'help,' but now it doesn't phase me. As a sidebar, only people who are serious about moving forward will actually fill out the form.

2. **3-Way Call Form -** If you have a home-based business, or perhaps are in a form of sales which requires that you do closing calls, the '3-Way Call Form' will absolutely help you become more efficient. This form is generated by the person who is asking you to do the call. Like the 'Request for Assistance Form,' this is submitted 24 hours before the call is to take place.

   There are several benefits to utilizing this, including the fact that it allows you to do research prior to the call. This is essential, especially if you are going to be talking to someone who has purchasing power and a sphere of influence. It is business etiquette to know your potential customers inside and out before you have the initial conversation. In today's world there is ample competition for what you do, and time and again, client service is going to win out.

People will often choose doing business with people they like even if these people are coming in at a slightly higher price. Take Starbucks, for example. When we order a drink, the server writes our name on the cup. The barista makes our beverage, which often costs more than the competitor, then loudly announces our name and order, 'Americano for Susan.' People enjoy hearing their name, and they also enjoy personal touches. By being prepared for important calls, it allows us to do our homework and create a fertile environment for the sale.

The 3-Way Call Form has the following components:

- Name and Phone Number of Person Requesting the Call
- Name of Potential Client

- Personal Information
    o Approximate age
    o Family
    o Hobbies
    o Profession
    o Website
    o Facebook/Social Media
- Time of Day Requested
- Primary Interest (example – if you are in health and wellness – weight loss, energy, etc., or let's say you sell cars – luxury SUV, economy, etc.)
- Information Viewed (website, brochure, etc.)
- Any other information.

When I receive this form, all details are calendared, and I take time to view the information that is sent over. If this person is a VIP, I will make an extra effort to Google™ them and click on the 'NEWS' tab to see if they have recently received any press. When it comes time to have the call, I am prepared. Let's say I found out that this person had received an award from their local Rotary Club. I might say something like this, *John, thanks for taking time out of your busy schedule. In preparation for this call, I wanted to be respectful and make sure that I could serve you to the best of my ability. I happened to find out that you recently received an award from Rotary. That is a huge honor. Congratulations.'*

People like when you make an extra effort. By preparing in advance, you are also able to keep these calls to 15 minutes. Since I started doing this, my closing rate has improved dramatically. Because I am able to limit calls to 15 minutes, I am also able to get more done.

Web-Based Request Forms

There are several options when it comes to creating web-based submissions forms, and it ultimately comes down to which platform you are using. I suggest you Google™ 'web-based submission widgits' and then say, 'for Infusionsoft™, Word Press™,' or whatever online platform you are using. Many businesses use a web-based submission form so that they can organize client communication and furthermore limit the amount of verbiage they are dealing with.

If you do not have a business, do not think web-based submissions aren't for you. Many parents use online programs such as Sign-Up Genius™, Survey Monkey™ and Evite™ as a way to volunteer, survey other parents about an upcoming event, or host a party. All of these are considered online form-style layouts that can make life easier.

If you are creating your own submission form for a business, think about what you want the communication to accomplish. For example, if you are a speaker, you may have a form for potential clients to hire you. If you have a home-based network marketing business, you may have a form that people can use to make an inquiry about your opportunity. Most forms can be delivered via email in real-time, which allows you to follow up right away.

What Is the Next Step?

When communicating with anyone, there is always a call-to-action; inherently – what is that next step? Will they hear back from you? If so – when? Will they receive follow-up communication? If so – how? Whether you are building a sales funnel, organizing a massive fundraiser, or streamlining your communication, it is imperative that a person feels certain of how to proceed.

Auto-replies and auto-responders can be very helpful. An auto-reply can easily be set with an email. It simply lets people know that you are unable to answer their email right away. All email auto-replies should be short and provide clarity on the next step. An email auto-reply can also be useful if you do not want to return from your vacation and find a thousand emails awaiting your response. There are three great options for dealing with this:

1. **Set your email to auto-delete messages as they come in.** This is NOT a good idea if you have client sensitive emails, but it can be great for people who receive numerous personal emails. Your auto-reply could say something like this:

   "Thank you so much for connecting with me. My family and I are away enjoying some R and R. Would you please message me back on June 10th, after I return."

   This implies that you are not going to read the email and instructs people to contact you back. I love this because it also deals nicely with people who come to you for answers instead of seeking them out themselves.

2. **Give an alternative.** If you are able, having a buffer such as a full or part-time assistant is great. This provides people with an option if they cannot reach you. Your reply can say something like this:

"Thank you for reaching out. I am presently out of the office. If this is urgent, please contact Maria at xyz@abc.com."

or

"Thank you for connecting. If you receive this message, please feel free to text me at 888-888-8888 as I am traveling."

3. **Leave Your Auto-Reply On ... Always.** My friend, human empowerment coach, Jairek Robbins, has his auto-reply on at all times. He lets people know that he only returns emails once per day. Doing this can be effective, but if you are not going to stick to it, I do not recommend it. Your auto-reply may say something like this:

    "Hi and thanks for reaching out. Your email is important to me. To be the most productive, I return emails between 2:00 and 3:00 p.m. P.S.T. I look forward to getting back to you."

This strategy has helped many people streamline their communication. I teach my students that when we attempt to work on a project, like writing this book, for instance, and return emails at the same time, we are effective at neither. Regardless of which method, embrace the auto-reply.

Auto-responders are web-based applications that create some form of call-to-action for a user. An example would be when someone registers for your email newsletter and receives a confirmation form. Auto-responders are also key to building out sales funnels. When a person downloads a free e-book, as an example, they are now put in a follow-up sequence of communication.

The first email they receive may be a video from you asking how they are enjoying the e-book. The second email may be an offer to purchase a lower priced item. The third email confirms that purchase. A fourth email is a video from you asking them about the purchase and thanking them. The fifth email offers a higher priced product, and so on. Some of the best internet based marketers have become geniuses at this, effectively creating sequences that propel users to the next purchasing level, while creating sizeable profits for themselves in the process.

Auto-responders are not just for business owners. These can also be used for fundraising campaigns and other forms of charitable work. The most important thing to remember is that each part of the sequence must have a definitive call-to-action letting the user know what to do next.

Time It!

I can often be seen wearing my trusty Timex Ironman™ watch. I have worn the same type of watch for about thirty years. It is not just because I am a runner; it is very useful for my productivity. I have learned to time everything, especially when it comes to communication.

In Donald Trump's book, *Think Like a Billionaire*, he writes of a person who wanted to do a deal with him. This man contacted Trump's office repeatedly. Finally, Mr. Trump relented and said, "You have got three minutes." Instead of shying away from such a daunting task, Ricardo Bellino prepared relentlessly until he was able to deliver his salient points in one hundred and eighty precious seconds. Trump was impressed and decided to do business. This became one of the fastest deals in history.

In building a network marketing business, I have done thousands of calls over the years. In fact, I have every single one of them written down in notebooks. Initially, when I was just getting started, my calls were up to an hour. It was ridiculous. I realized that with that length of time I wouldn't be able to get as many done. I began to time my calls and focus on getting to the point faster. Today, all of my calls are booked in fifteen minute blocks, and people know that they must come prepared.

I also time my meetings. Face to face meetings are great; however, they use up valuable time. There is the preparation time – for me, this means hair and make-up as well as the commuting time. Whenever possible, I replace live meetings with virtual ones. This allows me to get more done and be much more effective. . A final note on meetings is to be extremely clear on the front end in terms of exactly how much time you have. People prefer professionalism, and as you learn how to respect your own time, others will too.

As you begin to time yourself, you learn how to become more efficient, and in business, efficiency is key. I read that Jessica Alba, one of the founders of The Honest Company and well-known for her movie roles, initially went to investors with a lengthy PowerPoint presentation and an even longer pitch. They didn't go for it. Her next pitch was much more streamlined, had a singular focus, contained only ten slides, and guess what? They invested. Today, Jessica Alba is well on her way to becoming a billionaire. Ms. Alba learned how to become more time-efficient and value the time of the audience that she was pitching to.

Ask yourself where you can become more time-efficient? How can you communicate more effective time boundaries? Can you say what you want to in less time? Can you deliver a powerful message with passion, using fewer slides or visual aids? Are you able to identify where your communication may be losing effectiveness?

Pastor Joel Osteen has over seven million viewers in twenty plus countries that tune into his 'Message of Hope' every week. In the categories of Christian Broadcasting, personal empowerment and human development, he is arguably one of the most followed people of our time. I have read that he spends days working on one thirty minute message that he delivers usually three times on a Sunday. All of his messages follow a certain recipe – a greeting, a joke, painting the picture of a problem, providing a solution and then reinforcing the message with one or two key passages from the Bible, followed by a story. He has discovered that thirty minutes is the optimal length of time that people can remain focused and attentive.

'Ted Talks' are another great example of streamlined communication. The average 'Ted Talk' is about eighteen minutes, and the good ones receive millions of views. Mega trainers like Simon Sinek and Dr. Amy Cuddy have literally had their careers reach a meteoric rise due to one eighteen minute speech. Many of the events at which I speak are now heading toward a 'Ted Talk' style format. This has been well-received by audiences who like the fast-paced format. As a speaker, like Joel Osteen, I have been forced to deliver a powerful message in a shorter period of time, getting rid of redundancy. Thus, I practice over and over again to ensure I can wisely use my time.

I would encourage you to start timing everything. Time your calls. Time your meetings. Time yourself in all aspects of your life. We can all become more efficient with our time, and ultimately, becoming highly effective with our communication and creating time boundaries will help us liberate ourselves to spend our time doing more of what we love.

Does Multi-Tasking Work?

The wealthiest people on the planet are keenly aware of how long it takes them to do something. They are also masterful at multi-tasking. I witnessed this in person while spending a couple of hours with designer Donna Karan. We were in her downtown studio. She was getting her make-up and hair done for a photo shoot, confirming design ideas and also returning phone calls. She did not waste a minute. Ms. Karan sold her company to LVMH in 2001 for a reported $450 million and is now helming her new project, Urban Zen.

In business and in life, it is essential that we embrace the ability to multi-task. Like Donna Karan, we must be able to effectively squeeze as many things into our productivity time as possible if we are to create more time for the important things like family, exercise and rest. In my own life, I am an intense multi-tasker. Any time spent in the car, when I do not have children with me, is used to return phone calls. I have been known to do dinner prep while chatting with one of my staff. When my children were little, I also did three-way phone calls while changing diapers as I grew my multi-million dollar network marketing business.

Yes, there is an argument as to whether multi-tasking is possible; however, I would suggest that it is essential to success. Whenever we can combine two activities that are both vital to progress, it is a healthy use of time. Other ways in which I multi-task are to meet with potential clients for a powerwalk instead of lunch – thus, we are exercising and meeting. I also exercise and listen to personal empowerment and financial audios – I am learning and working out. In today's fast paced world, things are speeding up. As someone who teaches balanced living strategies, it is imperative you understand that to create more balanced moments in our lives we will have to double up wherever we can.

Ask yourself where you can combine two activities, even if it is as simple as commuting and making phone calls or meeting with a business associate and working out. As an aside – how many deals are done on a golf course or over a meal? Two essential activities combined - people doing this may not think they are multi-tasking, but they absolutely are.

I know that you can become more productive, have greater time efficiency and streamline your communication. As you do this, you will find you have much more time to do the things that really matter, and ultimately, achieve more of those balanced moments and truly live into the woman or man that you have always wanted to be.

Organize Your Life Now

1. Create a professional email signature.

2. Clean up your emails.

3. Create a web-based intake form for communication.

4. Choose virtual meetings as much as possible.

5. Let people know in advance how much time you have.

Chapter Seven
Who Earns Your Time?

*"Joy is what happens to us when we allow ourselves
to recognize how good things really are."*

-Marianne Williamson

We Can't Be All Things to All People

In my early twenties, running a health club, appearing five days a week on a local television show, guest appearing on radio, writing, training clients, teaching college, racing elite-level triathlon and attempting to be a good mother and wife, I burned myself out. As absurd as it sounds, and looking at the list of roles I had assumed, there was a strong belief that not only could I handle it all, it was essential for me to be all of these things to portray the image that I thought would cause people to accept me. It was a delusion; no wonder I ended up getting sick.

My biggest challenge wasn't 5 a.m. workouts or lesson planning for my students; it was that I felt that I had to be all things to all people. Even in my health club, I assumed the roles of manager, fitness instructor, personal trainer, front desk person, sales associate and more. Looking back now, of course I became exhausted, and naturally, in my attempt to please everyone, I ended up disappointing a lot of people, especially my sweet little daughter, Avery. In business, this is a surefire way to self-destruct, and I learned it the hard way – losing everything.

People who are highly disorganized, perhaps taking on the persona of Helen-Helps-A-Lot, tend to do this; they are inclined toward people pleasing. On the outside, it may appear as though these individuals are superhuman; however, trust me, from experience, there is chaos below the surface, and if the behavior continues, there are some very likely outcomes – illness, loss of relationship, and bankruptcy.

I have observed this with my students. They tell themselves that doing more, and being more to others, will help them become successful. On the contrary, saying 'yes' to everyone and trying to be everything is counter-productive. Much like the chapter where we learned the art of saying, 'no,' we must embrace the notion that when it comes to the roles we assume and the people we choose to spend our time with, less is definitely more.

Retrospectively, and our vision of the past is often crystal-clear, I would have been much better off relegating myself to fewer roles, delegating more and identifying the key people in my life who were most important, cultivating those relationships and working strategically with my network to see how I could streamline and improve. In this section, we are going to develop a high degree of clarity in terms of who qualifies for your time and which relationships garner more attention. Furthermore, in our Life Hack Section, we will look at the 5 Principle and list out ideas that you can implement right now to fortify strategic alliances in your business and personal life.

Who Is Going to Cry At Your Funeral?

I once read that, on average, only four people cry at a funeral. In my class, my students are presented with the idea that if someone isn't going to cry at our funeral, they do not earn the right to an opinion over our lives. Think about this right now – do you run around trying to please people that you know full well would not be there in a crisis? Do you assume many roles, perhaps volunteering for things you do not want to do in order to garner some form of acceptance? If you truly want to be organized, balanced and productive, you will have to embrace the notion that you are not going to please everyone and that the relationships that are most important are those that elicit a connection that is mutually beneficial.

We Have Two Choices When It Comes to Our Relationships

Have you ever been entangled in a conversation, fighting the urge to check your watch, finding every second painful and a complete waste of time? Have you ever made yourself overly available to people, thinking that you needed to be, only to end up resenting others, and yourself, because you were riddled with guilt at taking the call, or the meeting, when you knew there were other priorities? Who hasn't?

The reality is that if we want to be productive, balanced and feel fulfilled, we cannot be available all of the time. We may have the deep-rooted desire to be nice, to indulge our sister who is yet again complaining about her marriage or the business associate who is whining that they are not getting results. However, when we spend time with these people, we are not spending our time in the areas that mean the most.

I coached a woman once who was overwhelmed, exhausted and frustrated. She was gaining weight and not sleeping at night. She had two young children and a thriving network marketing business. She lamented that her phone started ringing early in the morning and continued late into the evening. People were interrupting her family time, and her husband was beginning to become resentful. I asked her a simple question, "Why are your picking it up?"

Initially, she was perplexed, responding that she needed to in order to do business. My next question was this, "Do you have hours of operation?" She did not. She had decided that she needed to be available to everyone all of the time. Again, I posed another question, "So what is this costing you?" She knew, in her heart, that her family was suffering.

The advice I gave her was this – set hours of operation, get a separate phone line for business and create some boundaries. We went through her schedule, and we blocked out meal times, a special night for just her and her husband, time for her to produce and time for her to unwind. My mentor, the late Jim Rohn, said, *"Six days on and one day off."* We chose her one day off.

This woman was highly coachable and did everything I suggested. Just a week later, I received a phone call. She was doing much better, her husband and kids were happier, and even though she was not as available, her business had already started increasing. I was not surprised. What my client had done was take a posture in her life, carve out time that was dedicated to those who were most important and educate her sales associates as to when she was and was not available. A further benefit was that she was now fostering respect and admiration from her team.

Earlier in this book, we discussed the biggest regrets of the terminally ill; not allowing one's self to be happy was one of those five. If your personal interactions are not making you happy, you have two choices – either improve the relationship or limit the time you spend with the people who do not bring you joy by creating boundaries. Productive, fulfilled people do not waste precious moments with people who tend to rob them of energy, and they seek to constantly improve the relationships that are the most important.

Make a decision right now to create some boundaries. In previous chapters we worked on scheduling. Whether you record a voicemail with your office hours, list them on your email signature, post them on your office door, or whatever it is that you have to do – be clear about when you are and when you are not available. This will liberate you, and the moment you begin living into these boundaries, you will begin to respect yourself more, and thus, others will do the same.

The Relationship R.O.I.

Think about all of the people in your life – your family, your friends, colleagues, social media connections and your local Starbucks Barista; when it comes down to it, in today's world we have relationships with a great many people. I once heard that by the age of thirty, we have encountered a minimum of three thousand people. With social media, that number is likely quite a bit higher.

Not all of our relationships are lasting; some are fleeting interactions while other people are in our lives for a season or more. Some people remain close to their best friend from kindergarten while other people grew up living in many places, not really creating long-standing friendships. Regardless of the duration or intensity of our interactions, one thing remains constant – each relationship has an R.O.I. – a return on investment, and it is either positive or negative.

The term R.O.I. is often used when it comes to portfolio management and business ventures. Inherently, we want to use our money to create more money. In our relationships, once we truly understand the value of our own time, we want to ensure that as many of our human interactions as possible have a positive R.O.I. for both ourselves and the other individual. This means resisting the urge to take negative actions against someone who is doing something which we perceive to be negative to us.

From an organizational standpoint, think of it like this – if we are wasting our time ruminating over negative people or spending time with them, we are not valuing our time, nor are we being productive. My students spend a week organizing their relationships by taking a long, hard look at where they are, not allowing themselves to invest time with people that do not serve them.

Thus far, we have learned the art of saying 'no,' and we have also learned how to streamline our communication. In this chapter, we will focus on how to make the most of the relationships that are most important to you and create a stronger R.O.I. by getting organized, structured and focused. You, and the people you care about the most, deserve the very best when it comes to emotional fulfillment. By using the strategies outlined in this chapter, you will elevate your relationships and perhaps even attract new people into your life who will help you get to that next level.

Your M.I.P.'s

M.I.P.'s stand for Most Important People. A woman I had coached was asked to make a list of the most important people in her life and consider, deeply, what it was costing her to not invest in these M.I.P. relationships while she built a business that was allegedly for the greater good of the family. I had also suggested to her that her top producing sales associates deserved more of her time than those who were coming to her to whine and complain. By using the techniques outlined in this book, she transformed her results because she embraced the notion that M.I.P.'s always get priority.

So how do we identify our M.I.P.'s? I want you to imagine for a moment that it is your 100th birthday. As you are seated in front of your cake, you are surrounded with the people you love and cherish the most. Looking around – who do you see? More importantly – who do you not see? The people we want to be surrounded by are those that we love and cherish the most. These are our M.I.P.'s, and in order to have beautiful, fulfilling relationships, we have to invest in them; and because time is finite, it is up to us to selectively make decisions on how we can spend more quality time with the people we care about the most.

The people in our lives who mean the most to us are, sadly, also the ones that we tend to take for granted. As an example, you may love your spouse; however, after giving one hundred percent at the office all day, you come home, barely say 'hello,' and quickly pour yourself a glass of wine and retreat into the study. You love your kids, but you barely see them because you are working so much. Perhaps you have a great friend who is always there for you, but you can't remember the last time you asked him or her to go out and do something fun. Life gets full, and the people we care about the most can end up going by the wayside because we do not make a concerted effort to invest in those relationships.

Conversely, there are those people in our lives with whom we know we are spending too much time, and the relationship is very draining. Your friend called complaining about her marriage for the fiftieth time, and as a result of you listening to her for an hour, you didn't sit down to play with your daughter as planned. Your colleague went on and on about your boss, and as a result, you got behind at work, had to stay late and missed date night with your partner. You spent an hour on the phone with a person in your business who was lamenting everything that was wrong in her life, and as a result, you missed your workout. Spending too much time with people who are not our M.I.P.'s borrows from the time you could be investing to do the things that bring you joy. Believe me, I have done all of these things only to end up resentful.

One of my dear friends was diagnosed with Stage Four cancer at the age of forty-seven. A father of two young children, a husband and business owner, he was sadly given only ninety days to live. As news spread of his illness, people who he hadn't spoken to in years suddenly wanted to come visit him or at least talk to him on the phone. His first thought was, 'you haven't been in my life, why would I want you in mine now just to appease your guilt.' Instead, my friend decided to only spend time with his M.I.P.'s; if there were only going to be ninety days, then why waste them.

People were nicely told, "Thanks but no thanks" for your desire to visit. Calls and texts were simply not returned. With the clock ticking, even spending valuable time away from his children and wife seemed improvident. During this time, we were in his M.I.P. circle. My objective was to do things that helped my friend find joy and also things that would fit into his new routine, which included rounds of chemotherapy and weekly visits to the doctor.

My friend had decided that he would walk two hours each day. Living in Canada, this meant many snowy, blustery, sub-zero trudges; however, he knew that this would be important for his therapy. I suited up in my huge, black, mammoth full-length ski coat and braved the elements with him. We laughed, we reminisced, and most importantly, we talked about the power of choosing who merited one's final days. He did not die after ninety days, and at the writing of this book, is still charging on. He does not waver on his M.I.P.'s and has said, without hedging, that life is too short not to spend time with the people we love the most.

I want you to think about your M.I.P.'s. If you, like my friend, were given only ninety days to live, who would you want to spend that time with? In this chapter, we are going to focus on M.I.P. relationships in five categories. The objective is that once we define who our M.I.P.'s are, we can use *Organize Your Life* strategies to help to strengthen and develop these cherished relationships.

Category One - People Who Live With You

Although the people under your roof may drive you crazy from time to time, they are there for a reason. These relationships may be harmonious or they may be lacking synergy. Either way, list out the people who live in your home here.

1.

2.

3.

4.

5.

6.

Category Two - M.I.P. Family Members Who Do Not Live With You

In this category, I want you to make a list of the top five family members who you want to get to know better, spend more time with, are curious about, or with whom you already have loving relationships. If you do not have extended family, perhaps there are people in your life who are like family—they could include godparents, 'aunties' and 'uncles' you had as a kid, or longtime family friends.

My friend, Karen, is the godmother of my kids. Her daughter, Chelsea, chose to take a gap year between high school and university. She didn't feel ready to make a decision about what she wanted to study and instead resolved that she would spend the year traveling to connect with relatives that she wanted to get to know better. She would travel all over North America, spending time with family members, learning about their lives and in turn, developing a deeper understanding of herself.

If you could really cultivate five external family relationships with people – who would they be? List them here.

1.

2.

3.

4.

5.

Category Three - M.I.P. Friends

This category is for your closest friends, people who you know have your back and you have theirs. These people uplift you, ground you, re-focus you and are greatly supportive. In my book, *The Have It All Woman*, I wrote about T.U.A. people in our lives. These are people with whom we have Total Unconditional Acceptance. We love them in good times and bad, we do not judge them, and in turn, they reciprocate those same sentiments back to us.

In my life, I am blessed to have a handful of T.U.A. M.I.P.'s. I know they will defend me, love me and would even take a bullet for me. These relationships have developed over time, and yes, some of the people who I initially thought were T.U.A.

M.I.P.'s turned out not to be which is absolutely fine because as we go through life, we have the opportunity to become more discerning.

If you do not have friends with whom you have T.U.A., then use this category to list friends who you'd like to have T.U.A. relationships with.

1.

2.

3.

4.

5.

Category Four - M.I.P. Business Associates

Even if you have a large company, there are still only a handful of people that you know you can absolutely trust. They may be in management, team members, co-workers, mentors or your best clients. In this category, there is some financial linkage, and developing these relationships can lead to promotions, synergistic business deals, increased revenue or even the inspiration for you to grow your ideas and monetize them.

Yes, in business, we all have lengthy Christmas card lists,

contacts, and so forth; however, I want you to imagine that you had to start a new company, and you could only have these five people to make it work – who would they be? List them here.

1.

2.

3.

4.

5.

Category Five - Your M.I.P. Network

My mentor, multi-millionaire and author of seven *NY Times*™ Bestsellers, Harvey Mackay, once said that if he lost everything tomorrow, he would make it all back within two years as long as he had his network. Your M.I.P. network includes people of influence, people who know how to get things done and are willing to help. In this section, I want you to write a list of five of the most powerful, influential people you know. These are the top people in your network, and outside of your family, this is the list you want to cultivate the most.

List the top 5 people in your M.I.P. network here.

1.

2.

3.

4.

5.

Now that you have this list of twenty-five people, ask yourself, 'How satisfied am I with these relationships?' Are there some relationships that are stronger than others? Are there people on the list that you want to be closer to, and yet, there is somehow a distance? Understand that every relationship can improve, regardless of how good it is, and all relationships, much like a garden, require constant cultivation and care.

In the following section, we are going to work on strategies to help to create more fulfilling relationships using five-minute strategies. You will be amazed at how powerful your associations can become when you make a concerted effort to invest in your M.I.P.'s. If you want a life of significance, balance, productivity and fulfillment, you learn to prioritize your M.I.P.'s. If someone isn't on one of these lists, ask yourself why you are spending time with that person. If there is some mutual R.O.I., then it makes sense. If the interaction is going to leave you feeling drained, angry and frustrated, why would you invest time knowing that you are taking it away from someone you genuinely want to be with?

The 80-20 Rule

In 1896, Italian economist, Vilfredo Pareto published a paper on landowning discrepancies in Italy. He pointed out that 80% of the land was owned by 20% of the people. Later, economists, sociologists and business strategists would base much of their hypotheses on the simple notion that 80% of results in an area can be attributed to 20% of the people. In building both traditional and network marketing businesses, it would be my observation that the same rule could be applied. Whether applied to sales volume or gross revenue, a handful of people are responsible for the majority of cash inflow.

In life and in business, it can be our tendency to overlook our top producers, or contributors, in favor of seeking out those whom we feel need our help. By doing so, we are forgetting about the people who are truly producing, perhaps telling ourselves that they do not require any recognition, contribution or upliftment. A little parable I teach to emphasize this point goes like this: *There was vineyard owner who had two large parcels of land.*

He tilled the soil, planted the seeds and tended to the young plants. For some odd reason, one vineyard began to thrive. The plants were stronger, greener and produced more fruit than the plants in the other vineyard. Although the owner was delighted with his crop in one vineyard, he was frustrated and perplexed about his other plants. He came to the conclusion that he must spend all of his time with the vineyard that was not producing.

He lovingly tended the vines. He watered and fertilized the plants. Day and night, he worked in the vineyard until it too began to produce fruit. 'There,' he said, 'now I have two healthy vineyards. Let me go and celebrate the bounty of my first vineyard also for now I will be very rich.' When he returned to his first vineyard, he was shocked to find that the plants had all withered and died. Instead of vines, heavy with fruit, there were withered leaves and shriveled grapes on the ground. 'How can this be?' he cried out.

The answer, of course, is that just because something seems strong and is producing does not mean that you stop reinforcing it. The story is used to teach the point that whether it is the child we have who is excelling in school or the sales team that is producing, we should never, ever take our top producers for granted. They may not require as much help as newer, or perhaps challenged people; however, we always want to make sure we are consistently fortifying what we already have.

Fortify Your M.I.P. Relationships

Whether it is scheduling time with your M.I.P.'s, creating special events for your top producers, remembering special occasions for the people on your list, or simply making a concerted effort to send a gratitude text, it should always be part of our daily method of operation to spend just five minutes reaching out to the people who contribute the most to our lives.

My daughter, Avery, had a friend who was going through a really tough time. She began to text her daily words of encouragement. Simple things like, "You have greatness inside of you," or "You are a winner." The girl was so touched with this simple gesture, and she asked Avery why she would do such a thing. Avery responded, "Because this is what my mother does for me."

Life can get hectic, and despite our best intentions, we can forget to let our M.I.P.'s know how we truly feel. One of the things that has been a constant in my own daily method of operation is to pour greatness into a minimum of three people every day.

Whether it is a quick text, an email, a Facebook message, a handwritten note or sending flowers, daily contribution is a part of my life as much as brushing my teeth or taking a shower. It takes me about five minutes to send these messages, and I have often received notes back saying, "You have no idea how much I needed this today."

Make sure you fortify your M.I.P. relationships every day. These are your 20% - the 20% who are contributing to 80% of the results you are receiving in your life. In the next section, you will find great ideas - things that can be done in five minutes to help to strengthen your relationships, your health and your finances. I would encourage you to embrace these five minute OYL Life Hacks and make them habit. As you begin to invest more into these key areas, watch how fast your results begin to radically transform.

Organize Your Life Now

1. Take a moment to consider if you are making yourself overly available to the wrong people?

2. Clearly communicate when you are available.

3. Make a list of M.I.P.'s in each of the categories.

4. Ask yourself who the 20% are producing 80% of the results in your life.

5. Write out a list of ways in which you can strengthen your M.I.P. relationships.

Chapter Eight
Keeping It Going

"Perfection is not attainable, but if we chase perfection we can catch excellence."

-Vince Lombardi

Awareness

Many of our students take *Organize Your Life* over again. In fact, we have almost a 70% returning student rate - something we are tremendously proud of. We do offer our students a highly discounted rate for taking our course again, and if you ask any of them why they do it, it comes down to one key reason – they want to keep their success going.

Once you embrace these *Organize Your Life* Principles and start leading a more productive, balanced life, you will not want to go back. Whether you start to generate more money, have a more fulfilling relationship or relationships, or get healthier, feeling focused and empowered becomes your new norm, and you do not want to go back to your old habits. Having strategies in place to stabilize your success is key.

In the beginning of the book, we covered awareness and the fundamental organization personalities. Simply being aware of your tendencies as you slide to the lower end of your spectrum is essential to maintaining new ways of being.

A young man attended a live event at which I spoke in San Diego. At 23 years old, he was entering the network marketing profession and wanted to make it his career. At the event, I trained on the personalities, and he resonated deeply with Militant Marty and Chaotic Carlos. He knew that he was wasting time making spreadsheets and also trying to be the life of the party – treating everyone to rounds of drinks. After that training, he was able to identify when he was going into those patterns and was able to course correct. One year later, he is more productive, saving more money and is much more organized. He credits having awareness as one of the key factors to his success.

To keep your momentum going, simply be aware of your patterns. This will be the number one contributor to your continued progress.

Use the 5 Principle

This, for me, is my saving grace to prevent overwhelm. When I have a day with a lot of things going on, I know that I can handle five. Whether it is putting on some old school eighties music and returning emails for five minutes, dealing with five pieces of mail, meditating for five minutes or working as a family to each find five things to donate, toss or recycle – five is very manageable.

To keep clutter at bay and productivity high, continue to ask yourself, 'What can I get done in these five minutes?' Another great question is, 'What five things can I accomplish right now?' If you are in sales, ask yourself, 'Who are five people I can set appointments with?' Five is so manageable, and in the last section on OYL Life Hacks, I will share 5 Principle Strategies in the three key areas of our lives – relationships, health and money.

Form a Tribe

Abraham Maslow's landmark work, *A Theory of Human Motivation*, published in 1943, proposed our own hierarchy of needs. After fulfilling our physiological needs, such as food and shelter, came safety and then love and belonging. Humans, it is proposed, are social animals that require some sort of tribe. I believe that one of the reasons so many of our students are successful is that for six concentrated weeks, they form a tribe online in a private forum. They share ideas, they uplift one another, and yes, they even confess to their organizational sins.

It is tough to maintain any new habit without support. Perhaps you do not have a high level of enthusiasm at home in terms of your new level of organization; however, that is not an excuse not to continue to keep up your efforts. Today, thanks to social media, we can connect 24/7. To stay the course, I would encourage you to plug-in. Sign up for our Balanced Living Weekly on www.stepintoyourpower.com, visit my Facebook Fanpage at www.facebook.com/susanslylive, go onto Pinterest and look at dream offices or other organizational inspirations for your home; most importantly, find your tribe.

Celebrate Your Wins

Sadly, many people go through life never giving themselves enough praise for a job well-done. Instead, it has been my observation that the majority of us seek external recognition for our efforts, and if this is the sole motivator, we end up disappointed. To maintain your success, it is essential to celebrate your wins. If you got your taxes done - jump up and down with excitement. If you got the monkey off your back – take a day off and bask in the glory of creating that clearing. Even little wins like clearing out your email in-box should be celebrated.

In Matthew 13:12, of the New International Version, it reads, *"Whoever has will be given more, and they will have an abundance. Whoever does not have, even what they have will be taken from them."* Essentially, one way to look at this verse is to understand that to those who appreciate what they have and give thanks for what they have accomplished – they will be given more. To those who do not appreciate their blessings and their victories – more will be taken away.

I used to be a person who was fearful of celebrating any victories because I had convinced myself that feeling accomplished led to complacency. Additionally, I created a belief that if I allowed myself to feel happy, something bad would happen. Many of our incorrect beliefs stem from childhood, and sadly, we grow into adults who hold those beliefs in such high accord that they supersede all else.

What I have learned is that the more grateful we are for the small wins, the more big wins come our way. When we can be happy for any progress, we bring to us greater levels of advancement. If you can allow yourself to celebrate your victories, big and small, and hold steadfast into this habit, you will soon find that more and more progress flows to you with greater ease.

At night, I tell my children the following and finish all of my talks this way. It seems only fitting to close the book with these lines as well.

You have greatness inside you.

You can be, do and have anything you dream.

You are a winner.

He who is within you is greater than he who is in the world.

OYL Life Hacks on Relationships, Money and Health

Five minute life transforming strategies to optimize your results.

What are 5 Minute OYL Life Hacks?

My students and clients become some of the most time-efficient people you will ever meet. They morph from disorganized, all-over-the-map, slaves to their lives into consciously competent individuals who like to make the most of every single day. In this section, you will find ideas, from both my students and myself, on how to make significant progress in the trifecta – relationships, health and money - all in five-minute blocks. It is my hope that you will use this as a reference, and if you have some great five-minute life hacks of your own, you will submit them to us at www.stepintoyourpower.com.

Relationship Hacks

Your Partner

Even if you do not have a partner, read on so you can be prepared for that perfect soul mate when they show up. Living with our partner can be the most rewarding and challenging experience of our lives. Divorce rates currently are at approximately fifty percent, and although many experts have theories as to why this is – financial stress, the other person stops taking care of them self, I would chalk it up to the fact that we stop showing one another value. From here, it is a slippery slope to apathy and resentment.

I have worked with many people over the years who tell me that they have stopped having sex or just aren't attracted to their partner any more. The first advice I want to give you is that you have to stop trying to change them and start focusing on what you can do to make the relationship work. Unless the person is being abusive, there can always be hope, and it comes down to taking responsibility for the improvement of the situation.

With this in mind, here are five things you can do in five minutes to begin to breathe some life into your relationship:

1. **Take Gary Chapman's 5 Love Languages Online Quiz** – www.5LoveLanguages.com - this will help you to discern how you and your partner want to express love. My students are required to do this, and it has helped many of them improve their relationship.

2. **Spend 5 minutes planning a date night**. Go out for a great dinner, a long walk, or check out your favorite jazz club. Date nights are essential to any relationship, especially one with kids, and if they are not planned, they don't happen.

3. **Spend 5 minutes taking turns at playing an adult version of Simon Says**. Dr. John Gray, a friend of mine, who endorsed The Have It All Woman, suggests that

couples spend a few minutes taking turns to tell their partner what they want. Sexually, our relationships can get into a rut, and if it is your intent to be with this person for decades, then it is imperative that you communicate in the bedroom.

4. **Send love texts to your partner every day.** You may also choose to write a note. Either way, we all want to be appreciated and daily notes are a wonderful way to let your partner know how much you truly love them.

5. **Look into one another's eyes and breathe for five minutes**. Yes, it may feel awkward; however, as William Shakespeare wrote, *"The eyes are the window to your soul."* When we look deeply into the eyes of another person, we create a profound connection. In workshops I have done, people doing this exercise have had incredible experiences, including seeing another person's childhood, feeling their emotions and being able to observe their thoughts.

Your Kids

If you have children, know that it is never too late or too early to nurture these relationships. I strive to teach my students techniques to enhance how they interact with their children regardless of age. Here are some life hacks to start right away with your kids:

1. **Sit down for dinner five nights per week.** A 2011 study from CASA (Center on Alcohol and Substance Abuse) Columbia found that teens who sit down for dinner with their family five or more nights per week were significantly less likely to abuse drugs, alcohol and nicotine. On Sunday night, plan out your meals for the week. Get your kids involved by including them in planning, meal prep and cleanup. Planning takes only about five minutes; meals take longer, but the outcome is definitely beneficial. In our home, with after school programs, we do not eat at the same time every night; however, regardless of what is going on, we do eat together.

2. **Lunchtime Love Notes and Texts.** Take five minutes in the morning and write out inspiring love notes on Post-It's for younger kids and text older ones. You may not

get a response at first, but trust me – if you stop – you will hear from them.

3. **You Choose!** Instead of always being the one to plan, simply say to your child, 'Let's do what you want to do right now for five minutes.' Read a story, color a picture, blow bubbles, build a puzzle...whatever it is – allow your child to be the boss. Remember – children have very little understanding of time. If all you have is five minutes, make the most of it, and they will love it.

4. **Schedule Individual Dates.** Pull out your calendar and schedule individual dates with your kids. Although family time is important, having that individual time is equally so. I might take one of my daughters for a nail appointment, another to a movie, and another to the mall. My son loves art, so a visit to Michael's is usually on his list. Whatever it is, we get out of the house to have our special time. Sometimes it is as simple as going for a hike or a walk. These dates do not have to be elaborate, but you do have to be present. My kids know that during these times, my phone is away and I am all theirs.

5. **The Job Board.** In our home, children do not get a set allowance. They earn their money. Each job around the

house has an agreed upon value. From unloading the dishwasher to bathing the dog, anything is up for grabs. When a child does a job, they give themselves a check. At the end of the week, the work is tallied and money is paid. It will take you five minutes to create a job board, and the lessons you teach your children about financial responsibility will last a lifetime.

M.I.P.'s

Our M.I.P.'s, whether family, friends, colleagues or people in our network, are important to invest in. Like any relationship – whatever we put in is what we get out.

1. **Research Favorite Sports Teams and Interests.** I make it a habit to learn the favorite sports teams of people in my M.I.P. business and network circle. If I want to send a special 'thank you,' I use a sports memorabilia service like Steiner Sports, out of New York, to send custom items to the people I do business with. This is a great way to get in the door of a desired contact and also to strengthen an existing relationship. I have sent a signed Peyton Manning lithograph to someone who is always there for me in business, a one-of-a-kind Mike Ditka photograph

to a Chicago fan and much more. Every time a recipient looks at something I sent them, they will remember the relationship. If you are in business, you definitely want to invest money into the people who you want to continue being in business with.

2. **Birthdays and Anniversaries.** My friend Ken is brilliant at this. He texts me on every single one of our family's significant days. Store this information in your phone, and be the first to send out a message. Many people will write on someone's Facebook wall; however, that often gets lost. A text or a call goes a long way. People so rarely send notecards these days, but an actual handwritten note is also a great way to go.

3. **For No Reason.** The old business adage – you scratch my back, I'll scratch yours, is so 1980's. Today, with so much selection, we cannot afford to be so selfish. Making a decision to send flowers or a bottle of wine, for no reason other than appreciation, is a powerful way to make a statement.

4. **An Exclusive Event.** If you have a sales team, group of employees, or people in your life that are on your M.I.P. list, create an exclusive event. In business, people may

have to qualify to get there; in your personal life, instead of throwing a party for five hundred, decide to contain it with the invitation, 'in celebration of the people we love the most.' Exclusivity is replacing sheer volume, and people love to feel special.

5. **Create a Group.** In business, having a preferential group of people who have benefits such as mentorship, training and exclusive events (as previously mentioned), can be very beneficial. Many companies do this – they create groups for people who have achieved certain production results. You can do this in a sales organization, for fundraising, donations and more. People love to belong to something special, and a group that one has to earn their way into can also create some healthy amplification of current production.

Health Hacks

When we are under stress, one of the first things to go is our health. The old idea of 'just exercise and eat right' no longer holds true. Many people who eat a fairly healthy diet and exercise five or six times per week still carry high levels of visceral, or toxic, fat. Factors that were recently not considered, such as toxicity, hormones, our gut biome (good versus bad bacteria), telomeres, the time of night we enter REM sleep and more, are contributing to the complexity of how healthy, or unhealthy, we are.

We live in a world where children die of cancer, and younger people have what were previously considered diseases of the elderly such as stroke, heart disease, Alzheimers, and others. I was only twenty-seven when I was diagnosed with MS, and at the time, I was exercising and eating a gluten-free, whole food diet. My case is not unique; having worked in the health and wellness industry for over two decades, these are things I hear about all of the time.

I would like to propose, from an organizational level, that when we are structured and managing ourselves in time optimally, we buffer stress to a higher degree; inherently, we make better choices. In this OYL Life Hack, I will share the five non-negotiables when it comes to our health and then add some extra tips from my fifteen year career as an elite personal trainer. Let's take your health to the next level.

The Five Non-Negotiables of Health

1. **Sleep -** A 2013 Gallup™ poll found that over 40% of Americans are getting less than adequate sleep. Health practitioners vary in terms of how much sleep they recommend; however, the 'gold standard' is a solid 7-8 hours per night. Science has discovered that sleep deprivation can lead to lack of focus, weight gain, hormone imbalance, decreased sex drive, depression and much more.

In order to live a balanced life, we must sleep. I used to be the person who thought I functioned well on five to six hours of rest. Nevertheless, I struggled to lose the last ten pounds, found myself irritable, lacking drive and motivation. When I started sleeping over seven hours each night, I felt happier, had more focus and a better quality of life.

To get your seven to eight hours each night, try the following tips that I recommend to my students:

i. **Shut down all screens one hour before bed.** Read a fiction book, journal, meditate, pray or do anything that relaxes you.

ii. **Create a calm environment in your bedroom.** My students paint their bedrooms neutral colors and take out any item that causes them to feel stress.

iii. **Remove all screens.** So many people fall asleep checking texts and wake up doing the same. It is NOT healthy. When my students take their phones and laptops out of their bedrooms, they start having more restful sleeps. I read a study which illustrated that children with televisions in their bedrooms had higher incidence of obesity. Screens are not for the bedroom - remove them whenever possible.

iv. **Black-Out shades.** This literally changed my life. Having blinds that create total darkness is tremendously beneficial, especially to those who travel constantly or those who work shifts. Make the investment!

v. **Natural sleep remedies.** As a society, we have become addicted to over-the-counter fixes when, sadly, there are so many good natural remedies out there. Chamomile tea is a wonderful sleep aid. Sip it one hour before going to bed. Melatonin, in small doses, has been found to have tremendous benefit. Some people find it comforting to have protein an hour before bed – a low carb protein shake that is high in L-tryptophan (a calming amino acid) can help to aid in sleep. Products rich in adaptogens can also be beneficial. Adaptogens are a group of naturally-derived organic materials that help our body buffer stress. Work with a natural health practitioner to find out what works for you. For my product recommendations, visit www.stepintoyourpower.com.

2. **Exercise.** We all know that exercise is vital to our well-being, and yet, according to the Centers for Disease Control, only 20% of Americans get the recommended 2.5 hours per week of cardiovascular exercise they require. The number one culprit isn't lack of desire – it is lack of time. Ultimately, we all know the benefits of exercise – better mood, sleep, increased sex drive, healthy weight maintenance and so forth; however, we are just not carving out the time to do what we know is good for us. Here are some ways to get that exercise and start creating better health right away. Ideally, you want to do more than five minutes of exercise, but if you are having one of those days where your time is limited, these short workouts can be done throughout the day to help you increase your fitness.

    i. **The 5 Minute Lymphatic System Workout.** The lymphatic system of the body is an integral part to waste removal. When things are 'backed-up' we can swell, feel tired and experience unnecessary stiffness in our joints. This is a great workout for people of all ages, and I suggest purchasing a rebounder (small trampoline) and doing this first thing in the morning. Start with a minute of gentle bouncing with your arms at your sides. Increase the intensity of the bouncing and bring your arms above your head and then down to your sides. Then do another minute of gentle bouncing, another minute of the intense bouncing with arm movements, and finally, a minute of bouncing and shaking your arms out in front of you.

ii. **The 5 Minute Resistance Workout.** We all have five minutes, and this short workout, done daily, can have great results. Do a minute of push-ups, a minute of sit-ups, a minute of squats, a minute of chair dips (for triceps) and a minute of lunges. When I travel, sometimes I have an early call time or flight. If I do not make it to the gym, I do this style of workout. It gets my blood pumping, and my philosophy is always – something is better than nothing.

iii. **The 5 Minute Interval Workout.** I recommend that this workout is done after you have been moving for a while, not as soon as you roll out of bed. Simply jog lightly for one minute to get warm. Then sprint for 30 seconds, jog for 30 seconds and repeat two more times. Cool down by jogging for one minute.

iv. **The 5 Minute Stretching Workout.** As we age we lose flexibility, not necessarily because we are getting older, but because we aren't stretching. I recommend doing this workout at night as you have had the entire day to warm up your muscles. Begin by standing tall (as if you had a book on your head) and take three long, deep, slow breaths. Bring your shoulders toward your ears and then drop them down. Repeat this three times. Next – extend your arms over your head and swan dive down until your hands touch the floor. You may have to bend your knees. With your hands on the floor, lift up slightly and look forward. Exhale and bring your head back down. Repeat this three times. Next – take your legs back and hold a 'plank' position. Drop your knees if necessary. Hold this for three long breaths. Next – drop all of the way down to the floor and bring your hips back with arms extended (child's pose) and hold for three deep breaths. Repeat the entire sequence one more time. The combination of breath work and active stretching can help release the low back and hamstrings.

v. **The 5 Minute 'All-Out' Workout.** This interval workout is best done when your body is warmed up. We hear a lot about the benefits H.I.I.T. (High Intensity Interval

Training), including accelerated fat loss, calorie burn and better overall fitness. Start by jogging fifteen seconds, sprinting fifteen seconds, jogging fifteen seconds and sprinting fifteen seconds. Then do twenty jumping jacks followed by twenty low squats (think about getting your bum to your ankles). Do twenty burpee jumps followed by twenty push-ups. Then jog fifteen seconds, sprint fifteen seconds, jog fifteen seconds and sprint fifteen seconds. Finish with five jumping jacks, five low squats, five burpees and five push-ups.

3. **Water.** Water is essential for flushing out toxins, increasing our mobility, and providing liquid that has numerous functions in the body. When we do not drink enough water, we can gain weight, feel a false sensation of hunger, get tired, anxious and much more. Here are five tips to get your water, aiming for approximately ten glasses per day.

   i. **Mix it with lemon.** Lemon will neutralize chlorine. If you take your non-BPA container with you, put a couple of wedges of organic lemon in it. When you fill at a fountain, the lemon will help to naturally filter your water.

ii. **Go Herbal**. Naturally decaffeinated herbal tea is a wonderful water substitute. Many of my nutrition clients, when I was practicing, preferred to meet their water quota this way, especially in the cooler months.

iii. **Carry It.** As a trainer, some of my clients included professional athletes who had a very high water quota. When they left their home in the morning, they carried their water for the day, aiming to get it all in. Yes, you may be slugging around containers, but when it is right there in front of you, you are much more likely to drink it.

iv. **Use a Crayon.** Another way to remember to drink your water is to mark, on a pint glass, each time you fill up. This way you will not forget how much water you have had.

v. **Space It.** We are all creatures of habit, whether we want to believe it or not. By simply having our water at the same time every day, we begin to get in the routine of meeting our quota. My clients, who were not previous water drinkers, quickly find that they feel much better getting adequate intake, and their bodies begin to crave routine. Start by having a large ten ounce glass first thing in the morning. Drink another glass mid-morning, another just before lunch, another after lunch, another two glasses spaced in the mid-afternoon, another an hour before dinner, and another after dinner. I do not recommend drinking too much water with meals as it can limit digestion.

4. **Nutrition and Supplementation.** Very simply – what we consume is the life we lead. If we put garbage in, we will feel like garbage. Here are five simple, easy to follow tips to improve your nutrition:

   i. **5 Servings of Fresh Vegetables and Fruits.** The Framingham Study found that consuming five to seven servings of fresh vegetables and fruits would reduce our risks of many of the leading diseases. This should be non-negotiable for every member of your family.

   ii. **Space Meals.** It takes our bodies about twenty minutes to register fullness, and when stress hormones are running high, we may not process the sensation until we are quite over-stuffed. Start your day with a protein-filled breakfast. In our home, we all have either vegan or whey protein shakes. Wait two to three hours and have a light snack - an organic apple and some raw almonds or perhaps an organic yogurt and a quarter cup of blueberries. Lunch should contain protein and vegetables. If you are having a grain, choose something slow digesting like organic brown rice. Mid-afternoon, have another snack of protein and a fresh vegetable or fruits – think hummus and organic celery or a hardboiled egg and some cut-up organic peppers, cucumbers, etc. For dinner, I recommend refraining from starches and loading up your plate with fresh vegetables and a protein.

iii. **5 Ounces**. Our body can only process approximately 30-32 grams of protein at a time. This amounts to about five ounces of chicken, fish, beef, or other animal protein. When we overeat, we end up having digestive issues, and these can lead to a host of other factors. Learn to consume only what you can digest.

iv. **Fiber.** Our body requires fiber to flush out toxins and balance our digestive system. Many people do not get enough fiber. Make a concerted effort to eat fiber with every meal. Berries, whole organic grains, and cruciferous vegetables all contain healthy amounts of fiber.

v. **The Power 5**. I am a big believer in supplementing to close any nutritional gaps. Our foods are not what they were years ago. Depleted soil and industrial agriculture practices have left many of our foods nutrient void. Always work with your practitioner to come up with a supplement regimen that is best for you. The following supplements are what I call the Power 5, and I never travel without them.

1. **Probiotic.** Imbalances in our gut have been linked to many diseases including depression, leaky gut, anxiety, weight gain and even attention deficit. Probiotics can be found in foods like yogurt; however, it isn't always practical to take this with you. A daily probiotic can help to keep our bodies in balance.

2. **Enzymes.** Digestive problems are a big plague in the world right now. Enzymes, taken before meals, can help your body break down your food and create an environment where you are absorbing more nutrients.

3. **Multi-Vitamin.** There are high and low quality multi-vitamins out there. I recommend looking for

those that are gender specific, easy to digest, and contain a good balance of vitamins and minerals. I also take a multi that is focused on hormone balance. Please visit my website for a list of recommendations.

4. **Vitamin D3.** Numerous studies are pointing to the risks of Vitamin D3 deficiency. Although our bodies produce natural vitamin D from sun exposure, those that live in Northern climates often do not get the recommended levels. In order to discern how much to take, ask your practitioner for a Vitamin D test – this is the only way you can adequately gauge it.

5. **DHA.** DHA, or Omega 3 fatty acid, generally comes from a marine source. It has been shown to protect our brain, improve joint mobility and even help maintain a healthy body weight.

5. **Prayer and Meditation.** Taking time in quiet is essential to calm our very noisy minds. Whether we are praying or sitting in silence, creating a place where we tune out the distractions helps to balance our body. A study by Helm, et al, published in the Journal of Gerontology, found that

people who had a daily practice of prayer and meditation lived longer, healthier lives than those who did not. Start by spending five minutes in the morning and five minutes in the evening going within. Focus on breathing, communing with God and allowing yourself to simply, 'Be.' If you want to create a deeper practice, visit my website, www.stepintoyourpower.com. I have created a guided meditation series called, *The Shift.* People have written to share incredible stories of success they have received due to listening. From quitting smoking after fourteen years to healing a shattered relationship with a parent to increasing income, *The Shift* has helped many people. It is available for download for only $3.97.

Money Hacks

Money is a massive topic and deserves an entire book, in and of itself; however, how can we organize our lives if we do not take finance into account? My students have found money, generated more money and ultimately taken responsibility for their assets and liabilities. In my class, students make wills, find out their C.P.Q. (Cash Positive Quotient), work on their taxes and much more.

The following five tips have been tested and proven by my students with exceptional results. We work on many money hacks, and these core five are a great starting point.

1. **Take Control of Your Taxes.** According to Sandy Botkin, CPA and former IRS Attorney, the average entrepreneur is spending much more on taxes than they need to. He and his team have created an innovative app that does everything from track mileage to provide cloud-based storage for expenses. Go to www.taxplan.taxbot. com today and download this software. Compatible on IPhone and Android technology, my students find that they start saving money right away and feel much more empowered. The app also comes with access to accountants that you can call-in and ask questions of. If it is indeed possible to use the words 'taxes' and 'fun' in the same sentence, TaxBot accomplishes this.

2. **Get Rid of Multiple Store Credit Cards.** One of the fastest ways to accumulate debt is to rack up charges on multiple credit cards. Go into almost any store these days and you are offered additional savings if you sign up for a store-specific card. The challenge is that small balances on multiple cards add up to a whole lot of debt. Furthermore, forgetting even a small payment can drastically affect your credit rating. Stick to two main credit cards, preferably with the ability to accumulate rewards. I suggest having an American Express™ Card that you are forced to pay off every month to reign in

your spending and another card, such as a Visa™ or MasterCard™, where you can carry a balance, especially if you are in business.

3. **Educate Yourself.** Spend a minimum of five minutes every day listening to or reading a book on money. My top five favorite titles are:

- *Rich Dad/Poor Dad* - by Robert Kiosaki
- *Think and Grow Rich* - by Napoleon Hill
- *The Alchemist* - by Paulo Coehlo
- *The Richest Man in Babylon* - by George C. Clasen
- *The Science of Getting Rich* - by Wallace D. Waddles

There are many great books out there, and the more you educate yourself on money, the more likely you are to generate more and keep it.

4. **Get Honest**. Debt can be emotional, embarrassing and an overwhelming source of stress. Consequently, it can also hold us back tremendously if we do not deal with it. I had a student once who had amassed $180,000 in debt on multiple credit cards and did not tell her husband. She was binge eating, not sleeping and barely functioning. She had started a network marketing business, and naturally,

it wasn't thriving because she was too consumed with living a lie that she could not focus on doing what it took to succeed.

My advice to her was to get honest - to first seek out three options for debt consolidation and a repayment schedule and then to get honest with her husband. By coming to him with possible solutions, as opposed to just the problem, she was able to illustrate that, although she had been grossly irresponsible, she was now owning her choices. They had the conversation, and of course, he was shocked and angry. The good thing was that he was happy that she had come to him with options. They consolidated their debt and took massive responsibility to begin paying it off.

Whether you spend five minutes every day really looking at your debt, your assets, reviewing online banking transactions or investigating debt consolidation like my student, dedicating daily time to financial transparency is critical. My students are taught to organize their finances, have the difficult conversations and do whatever it takes to take control.

5. **$5/day/week/month.** A 2013 report released on Bankrate.com and published online on CNN.com declared that almost two thirds of Americans are living paycheck to paycheck and have little or no emergency savings. As tough as this sounds (and this is coming from someone who was once in that situation and ended up living on her brother-in-law's sofa), you have got to save money. Whether it is $5 per day, per week or even per month. We can all find $5 somewhere.

My students are taught to open a separate savings account as part of getting organized. Ideally, they take 10% of what they earn and use that money to make more money by investing it. Some, however, take the class and are gravely in debt. In which case, they are still taught to save, but it may not be as much as 10% since that is likely not available.

Recessions, layoffs and emergencies happen. Going through life without a contingency fund of savings is irresponsible. I have been there myself and learned the lesson the hard way. Saving money is not easy – if it were, then everyone would be wealthy. The truth is that success comes from doing what is hard - the things that average people do not do. Start today with getting that savings account open and taking financial responsibility for your life.

References

1. Verma, Ragini. "Sex differences in the structural connectome of the human brain." Proceedings of the National Academy of Sciences. Crossmark, Dec. 2, 2013. www.pnas.org.

2. American Psychology Association. "Stress in America: Paying With Our Health." Feb. 4, 2015. www.apa.org.

3. Harris Polls. "Are You Happy? It May Depend on Age, Race/Ethnicity and Other Factors." May 30, 2013. www.harrisinteractive.com.

4. Eker, Harv T. *Secrets of a Millionaire Mind.* 2011. Print.

5. Skinner, B.F. 1930-1950.

6. Ware, Bronnie. "Top five regrets of the dying." The Guardian. Feb. 1, 2012. www.theguardian.com.

7. Baer, Drake. "Why 80 Percent of Your Emails Are a Total Waste." University of Glasgow. www.fastcompany.com. Aug. 14, 2013.

8. American Psychiatric Association. *Diagnostic and Statistical Manual: Mental Disorders.* 1952.

9. Rorschach, Hermann. *Psychodiagnostik.* 1921.

10. Hippocrates. 460 BC-370 BC.

11. Zimbardo, Phillip. "Stanford Prison Experiment." 1999. www.prisonexp.org.

12. Hadhazy, Adam. "Think Twice: How the Gut's "Second Brain" Influences Mood and Well-Being." Scientific American. Feb. 12, 2010.

13. Corley, Thomas. *Rich Habits: The Daily Success Habits of Wealthy Individuals.* March 1, 2010. Print.

14. Weiss, Robert. "How Much Sex is Healthy?" Huffington Post. 2014.

15. Ferriss, Tim. *The 4 Hour Work Week.* Dec. 15, 2009. Print.

16. Trump, Donald. *Think Like a Billionaire."* Mass Market Media. 2007. Print.

17. Mackay, Harvey. *Swim With the Sharks Without Being Eaten Alive.* Harper Business. Nov. 8, 2005. Print.

18. "You've Got Mail." Directed by Nora Ephron. 1998. Warner Bros.

19. Jones, Jeffrey. Gallup. "In US, 40% Get Less Than Recommended Amount of Sleep." Dec. 19, 2003. www.gallup.com.

20. Center for Disease Control, Division of Nutrition, Physical Activity, and Obesity. "How much physical activity do adults need?" Updated June 4, 2015. www.cdc.gov.

21. Helm, Hughes. "Does Private Religious Activity Prolong Survival?" The Journals of Gerontology. June 23, 1999.

22. Bankrate.com. "76% of Americans are living paycheck-to-paycheck." June 24, 2013. www.money.cnn.com.

23. Alba, Jessica. The Honest Company. Founded 2011.

24. Van Meter, Jonathan. "Ivanka Trump Knows What it Means to Be a Millennial." Feb. 25, 2015. www.vogue.com

25. Ted Talks. 2000+ talks to stir your curiosity. 1984-present. www.tedtalks.com.

26. Framingham Heart Study. Originally 1948. Revised 1971, 1994, 2003.

27. Osteen, Joel. Lakewood Church. www.joelosteen.com.

28. CASA Columbia. "2011 Family Dinners Report Finds Teens Who Have Infrequent Family Dinners Likelier To Smoke, Drink, Use Marijuana." Sept. 22, 2011. www. casacolumbia.org.

29. Maslow, Abraham. "A Theory of Human Motivation." Psychological Review. 1943.

Praise for The Organize Your Life Principles

"I owe a lot more to Susan than just learning her 5 principles and how they have assisted me. What I didn't realize is how impactful the 5 principles would be on my entire life. I have now applied them to everything I do. My day planner, my car, my closet, my work bag, and my personal daily routine. I have become more productive, more responsible, more focused, and most importantly more organized in my life. What wasn't clear was how much of a snowball effect this ends up having on you.

There is a psychological connection that takes place between organizing your daily planner and how that ends up bleeding into your entire life. It has been one of the most rewarding, satisfying, and incredible personal growth journeys I have ever been on. You may think you have your life organized, but you are immediately hit with a does of reality with Susan's amazing Organize Your Life course. Thank you, Susan, from the bottom of my heart for all you do and all you continue to do for me personally and professional as a friend and mentor."

Much Love, Respect, and Health,
Scott A.

"Because of your course (Organize Your Life), I have learned to prioritize, set a schedule (and for most part stick to it), and learned to say no (last weeks class) gracefully and tactfully. Thank YOU for being an amazing role model, mentor, friend. I appreciate you!"

Hugs and have a wonderful day!!!!
Casey J.

"So I am excited to share this victory! Even though my new house is not technically mine yet, I decided to act as if it is and create that relationship with the universe. I decided to apply for new jobs today in NJ. I applied for a position, and NO JOKE, in less than 1 minute... the person called back and offered me the job over the phone! I was like HUH?.... I emailed you literally 30 seconds ago! She said the email signature alone was so professional that she new she had to open up the resume and that the resume was so impressive she didn't even need an interview! I am opting to meet in person to make sure it is a

good fit and I am paid what I deserve but... I am so excited! It was in OYL I learned what an email signature even was! This is the ONLY class I have ever taken that I benefit from EVERY day of my life!"

Jessica L.

Acknowledgments

Profound gratitude, love and appreciation to my beautiful husband, and life partner, Chris, without whom I would not have been able to create this work. To my children – Avery, AJ, Sarai, Emery and Maggie – thank you for being a source of constant inspiration. To our team – Tisha, Gloria, Bre and fabulous editor, Joel – thank you for your unending support. To my OYL students – thank you for continuously challenging me to provide better and better content. To JJ and the team at Sound Concepts – thank you for always being as excited about new projects as I am.